HOW TO LAUNCH AN INTEGRATIVE PRACTICE

A step-by-step guide

Kelly J. Parcell, ND

NaturePub Press

This book is dedicated to Steve Parcell, ND.

My husband, business partner, colleague, friend, and teammate in this life.

We are more powerful together.

CONTENTS

PART II: How to Find the Best Place for You to Practice

PART III: How to Prepare to Open Your Practice

CONTENTS

CONTENTS

Afterword

HOW TO LAUNCH AN INTEGRATIVE PRACTICE

INTRODUCTION

If you're reading these words, you are probably considering starting your own integrative practice.

How are you feeling: optimistic? Hopeful? Excited? A little intimidated? A lot intimidated?

It's okay. You're not alone. That's why I decided to write this book, to help ease your fears and minimize intimidation. I promise, what you're thinking of doing is doable!

You have questions.

Maybe you've been in practice a long time. Maybe you're new to practice. Maybe you're somewhere in between. Whatever your level of experience, welcome. You picked up this book for a reason: you want to know if there's a better way to practice than what you're doing now.

You're probably wondering how difficult (or easy!) it might be to make the transition to your own operation. You're curious to know what's involved, if you have the skills and resources to take on the task, and how hard it is to get them if you don't have them already.

Most of all, you want to know how to make the decision and, if it's the right path for you, how to go about bringing it into reality.

What is an integrative practice?

An integrative practice is known by many names such as alternative medicine, complementary medicine, or healing-oriented medicine. They're all the same. The difference is defined by your focus, skills, and priorities.

I am a naturopathic doctor. From day one of naturopathic medical school, we learn that the body is connected as mind, body, and spirit. We are trained on the foundations of medicine as all medical students are in terms of anatomy, physiology, neurology, histology, biochemistry, psychology, and so forth. In addition, we learn about botanical medicine, homeopathy, nutriceuticals (dietary supplements), pharmacology, drug/nutrient interactions, intravenous therapy, psychology, manual therapy (basic manipulation techniques), hydrotherapy, and more. But most importantly we practice based on a set of principles that guides our approach to care. These principles unite those of us who practice in the alternative medical model:

The Healing Power of Nature (Vis Medicatrix Naturae): Naturopathic medicine recognizes an inherent self-healing process in people that is ordered and intelligent. Naturopathic physicians act to identify and remove obstacles to healing and recovery, and to facilitate and augment this inherent self-healing process.

Identify and Treat the Causes (Tolle Causam): The naturopathic physician seeks to identify and remove the underlying causes of illness rather than to merely eliminate or suppress symptoms.

First Do No Harm (Primum Non Nocere): Naturopathic physicians follow three guidelines to avoid harming the patient:
● Utilize methods and medicinal substances which minimize the risk of harmful side effects, using the least force necessary to diagnose and treat;
● Avoid when possible the harmful suppression of symptoms; and
● Acknowledge, respect, and work with individuals' self-healing process.

Doctor as Teacher (Docere): Naturopathic physicians educate their patients and encourage self-responsibility for health. They also recognize and employ the therapeutic potential of the doctor-patient relationship.

Treat the Whole Person: Naturopathic physicians treat each patient by taking into account individual physical, mental, emotional, genetic, environmental, social, and other factors. Since total health also includes spiritual health, naturopathic physicians encourage individuals to pursue their personal spiritual development.

Prevention: Naturopathic physicians emphasize the prevention of disease by assessing risk factors, heredity and susceptibility to disease, and by making appropriate interventions in partnership with their patients to prevent illness.

Naturopathic medicine is inherently integrative, bridging or "integrating" alternative therapies with conventional approaches. Whether your potential practice is one practitioner who has knowledge of alternative and conventional approaches or two or more providers who team up to offer both aspects of care, your practice will be an integrative practice.

But there's another aspect to consider, one that for most practitioners is the foundation of their interest. An integrative practice creates connections between approaches to patient care, but it's something else, too.

It's a practice that puts the patient at the center of care.

It's a practice where the mental, emotional, and physical health of the patient are primary concerns, never secondary.

It's a practice that calls on a hierarchy of treatment methods, beginning treatment with the least invasive measures.

As you can see, when I speak of an integrative practice, I'm talking about not just the practice of medicine but also our priorities of what we do. That's important, because a lot of things can crowd out our direct work with patients.

Having a practice requires dealing with insurance coverage, meeting (and fighting!) institutional quotas, handling pharmaceutical sales, and much more. An integrative practice cannot eliminate all those things, nor should it. Many elements of practice that do not involve direct patient care bring value to the process. The difference we find in an integrative practice is that we put priorities in their appropriate place – their best place, meaning that everything that is not directly related to patient care is secondary or lower, never primary.

Can I really start my own integrative practice with just this book?

Yes, you can.

That doesn't mean it will be as easy as a trip to the grocery to pick up what's on your list. But starting your practice doesn't have to be as difficult as you may be imagining it will be.

Yes, you'll need to learn to do things that may be unfamiliar.

Yes, you're still going to have to do things that have less to do with the practice of medicine and more to do with running a business and navigating third-party bureaucracies.

Yes, you'll be taking over several things that others are now doing on your behalf.

But it's a relatively short list of new obligations, and the benefits you will enjoy from taking them on will far outweigh the challenge of the learning curve to get there.

Even better, the time you spend on these new tasks will be more than compensated for in the additional time you will gain to spend with patients, to pursue other professional interests, or to have for your family, your friends, and yourself.

How do I know? I've been there myself, right where you are now.

Both my husband and I are naturopathic doctors (NDs). When we started our own integrative practice, we felt like we were treading in territory that no one had ever explored. Of course, that wasn't the case, but you wouldn't know it from the literature; rather, from the lack of literature. I found little encouragement and even less of what I needed most: experienced guidance on how to decide whether such a practice was right for us, how to launch it if we did decide to go ahead, and how to keep it going.

I decided that no one should be in the dark about how to do this, so I wrote this book.

Perhaps you are a naturopathic doctor just coming out of school, an ND going to a state where there are limits on your scope of practice, an MD, a doctor of osteopathic medicine (DO), an Advanced Nurse Practitioner (ANP) or some health-care professional. If you want to practice independently and you're interested in alternative medicine, this book will help you get started.

Filling the Knowledge Gap

When I went to school there was only one business class offered in my last year, and it delivered little in terms of tangible steps and practical guidelines for starting a practice. When we finally decided to launch our practice, my husband ended up meeting with a business consultant who told us the first thing we had to do was take out a $50,000 loan. (Spoiler alert! You don't have to do that. Which is another reason for this book: I'll dispel misinformation that may be interfering with your ability to choose what's right for you about starting a practice.)

I am not shocked at our lack of knowledge, but I remain shocked that the challenge of starting a practice remains such a "seat of the pants" endeavor, barely mentioned in medical school, let alone made a part of our education. Starting a practice is perhaps the most common goal among new graduates, but good luck finding even a weekend seminar in medical school to tell you how to do it. Just because so many doctors will work for an institution, hospital or established group practice doesn't mean everyone will. The impression I had at the time seems no different today. You gain a world of knowledge about medicine but the extent of how to handle the business side of it is not much more than Now you are a doctor – go do some doctoring.

Most of us who launch a practice end up figuring it out as we go along, relying upon instinct, observations, and luck. I started with an abstract of the practice I imagined, a business proposal that I created detailing the things I could think of that seemed important: estimating how many patients I would get over the first year, a mission statement, and some sample forms for insurance and payment plans. It was hardly complete. The reality was more complicated, and it included figuring out how to act on my desire to help people no matter their situation with the reality that if I didn't keep an eye on the bottom line, I would soon be out of business and unable to help anyone at all.

The good news is that I have come out the other side with a thriving practice.

The bad news is that I made a lot of mistakes along the way – mistakes that were costly in terms of lost income, lost opportunity, terrible inefficiency, time I didn't have to waste, and worry I didn't need to experience.

If only someone had given me some guidance at the beginning! That's why I wrote this book: to give back to my fellow practitioners on a matter that lacks the kind of support we all need.

I'm going to take you step by step through the things I wish I had known: the challenges, opportunities, and pitfalls that everyone encounters as they launch that new practice. I'll present it through facts and experience. Most of what's here I have yet to find written down or collected anywhere else.

There is no reason for anyone to have to start from scratch. My hope is that you find here exactly what you need to make the right decision about starting a practice, and, if you decide to launch, to make it just what you hope for.

PART I: How to Decide If an Integrative Practice Is for You

In this section, I'll help you figure out whether starting your own practice is right for you. Don't worry! We'll take it step by step.

Kelly's Experience

The spirit was in me to start my own practice, and honestly, that is what I always envisioned I would do. I never considered working for someone else. I knew I would go back to Boulder after medical school, hang out my shingle, and try to become what I thought might be a big fish in a relatively small pond. It did not seem too daunting, and I took one small step at a time. Having a partner to do this with was great because we could get so much more done as a team. The key to our success has been that we have a similar vision of what we want our practice – we call it NatureMed – to be and to become. We also have distinct areas of expertise. We identified each other's strengths and divided up the business needs accordingly.

In other words, we never had to do what you're doing right now, deciding if opening a practice is the thing to do, because we had never known a time when the idea wasn't a part of our thinking already.

If that's your situation, congratulations.

If that's not your situation, congratulations anyway, because this section will help you know your own mind about the matter.

And if your mind really is made up, I suggest you work through this part of the book anyway. Why? Because it will help you "know yourself" in ways that will help you as you work through the challenge of opening your practice. This section takes you through many matters of mindset and attitude, and it will be useful to have anticipated the challenges before they arrive – take it from someone who's been through it.

Uncertainty is a part of every new endeavor, but confidence is a choice. If you love this and want this, don't be dissuaded. Passion drives everything.

In business, you may fail or even go bankrupt, but if you love the work you're doing, you'll learn lessons for the next time around. Chances are that passion will limit the damage and error in the first place. This is what my parents taught me. My father started a few businesses out of his passion. One failed, but another grew to the top of its industry. Along the way he nearly went bankrupt twice and took many leaps of faith. When you follow your passion, the failures or hiccups are not obstacles but opportunities to grow. He taught me that if you love what you do, then work is part of your joy and not the thing you have to endure to get that joy elsewhere.

How to Use This Section

In this section of the book, you'll begin to think in detail about what you enjoy doing, what you're willing to do, what you won't do, and how to balance them toward making the right decision about opening your own practice. Treat each question as the springboard for your own reflection.

After each question is an exercise of several parts. Write down your reflections. Confine yourself to a paragraph or two. This will help you come to a succinct and focused conclusion, and help you avoid feeling overwhelmed. Just remember: a few sentences is plenty. All you have to do is read, respond, and keep moving ahead.

We'll begin by taking you through a series of questions divided into categories. Take your time. Make notes. Let your thoughts ruminate. The idea here is to shift your focus from the overwhelming question of "Should I take the leap?" to the smaller questions that can help you make that decision.

By working through the question of starting a practice, thinking about it one issue at a time, you'll not only arrive at the answer you seek, you'll have confidence that it's the correct answer for you.

Questions About You

Are you feeling fulfilled in your current practice?

Do you find your current practice fulfilling on a day-to-day basis? Have you wondered if there might be a way to conduct your practice that is more fulfilling?

These are not rhetorical questions. Some practitioners are perfectly satisfied with how they practice, and you might be one of them. If so, congratulations. But if you're sensing a lack of fulfillment, think about what in particular causes you frustration or even pain, and think about what might make things better. Some people are frustrated by, say, their morning routine of getting up and getting the kids off to school, but find that changing that routine can transform the experience from a burden to a pleasure.

Do you feel that there are things you could do better – that would make you happier – if you approached them in a different way? Do you feel rushed? Do you feel behind? Do you experience financial insecurity? Do you lack time to spend with friends and family? Is your own mental outlook dependent on that of your boss? Do you feel that you're not as far along in your career as you would like to be, or ought to be?

Maybe you work an eight-hour day, see 35 patients, and, at the end of the day, find yourself drained. Sure, your level of work may be keeping up the payments on your lifestyle, but you're doing so at the expense of working yourself to the bone. How much longer can you tolerate the schedule? How is your health? Are you the person you wanted to be as a doctor? Do you feel healthy and vital, with energy reserves for the rest of your life after you get off of work? Or do you feel like you're barely making it through the day?

Think about your fulfillment and write down your thoughts. Look for problems, but take stock of the good things, too. If you find that a "pros and cons" list will help, make one. Maybe you're already fulfilled in your work but you have yet to stop to realize that's the case. Maybe a few minor changes can get you to a better place. Or maybe you're not as fulfilled as you'd like to be and it's time for a significant change. Whatever the case, making a list of the particulars here will help you make decisions about what to do, including helping you decide whether to start your own integrative practice.

Exercise

1. Make a list of the pros and cons in your current practice. If you do not have a practice yet, describe what your ideal workday would look like. Start with when you wake up, go through the day leaving out nothing, and end with bedtime.

How do you feel about being your own boss?

Being your own boss has obvious benefits, but *having* a boss has benefits, too – benefits that might not be obvious until you're filling the boss' shoes. When you're the employee instead of the boss, that boss acts as a buffer between you and the world for certain kinds of disputes, many of which you never have to deal with because the boss handles them on your behalf.

When you are an employee, it's a given that you have to perform to the expectations of your boss, but ultimately you are not the final word on many matters. You work your shift and leave. If patients or employees are unhappy, it is only partially your problem. The doctor is often the one who gets all the credit even when the business of medicine hits a snag.

The boss knows where those snags are because the boss has to deal with them. If you're running your own clinic, everything that happens in the clinic reflects on you. Committed patients may give you the benefit of the doubt, but only to a point. If problems in the business or in care become a part of your image to the public, current and potential patients will often come to see this as a reflection not just of the clinic but also of you, personally. If you have colleagues in the clinic who are the source of the problem, you are still the boss. President Harry Truman had a sign on his desk that read *"The buck stops here."* If you run the clinic, that's going to be how people think about you.

As the owner, you will have to maintain your integrity not only as a practitioner but also as a business owner. When you are upset about something that has gone on in the clinic, whether it is the actions of another provider, a receptionist, or anyone else under your charge, how you respond is going to set the tone for everyone involved. You need to be the best you at all times.

That's not to say that the benefits are insubstantial. Far from it. Being your own boss means you can come and go as you please, you can use as much of your net profit in the business as you want, and many of your personal expenses will become business expenses that are tax deductible. You're going to gain flexibility in finance, decision-making, scheduling, service offerings, even the look and feel of the clinic. But you will have to be prepared for new and greater responsibilities. Are you prepared to handle them?

Exercise

1. Write down why you want to be your own boss.
2. Write down what you think will be difficult about the role, and what you think will be enjoyable.
3. In a single sentence, write down how you deal with criticism. Be specific.
4. Think about what you will do when you are confronted by patients on treatment, on payment issues, and on their disagreements with your professional judgment.
5. Consider two situations: your boss tells you to do something you don't want to do, or you're the boss and you have to force yourself to do something you don't want to do. Describe how you feel in each situation.

Are you comfortable having the last word in big decisions?

How comfortable are you thinking for yourself – signing off without someone above you reviewing things – on what treatment to give to a patient when you are free to make decisions without the red tape of hospital or insurance company policies?

When you are not restricted by the average seven-minute visit or an insurance company dictating what drug to give, you get to choose for yourself. Will you know what to do? What if you don't?

Once you start your independent practice, you can put the red tape behind you when it comes to patient care. Each patient that comes in can be addressed as you wish. You can take time to listen to their health concerns. You can ask questions and take as much time as you need. You can run whatever blood work or testing that you need to and take time to do the physical exam. You can listen carefully to the heart and lungs without the patient getting light headed as you no longer have to rush them through deep breaths. You can give them nutritional advice, supplement advice or even wait to write that prescription. You can not only give yourself time to figure out the best and comprehensive course of action, but you can give your patient time to practice health between visits. Patients are paying out-of-pocket and they want answers quickly. You can do more than just the basics right away on the first visit. It is your call!

Exercise

1. Name a professional situation in which you have second-guessed yourself. Did you eventually accept your choice? How long did it take? Did you change your mind later and reverse yourself with the person or situation it affected?
2. Write down what fears you have, if any, when you think about making significant judgments about treatment.

Are you able to "unplug" from work?

Can you step away for a few hours or even a few days on your own? Or does someone else have to talk you into taking a break? When you work for someone else, the decision is often made for you. But if it's your clinic, you'll need to be able to say "no" to more work – you'll need to be able to rely on yourself to set limits that keep you from exhaustion and burnout.

Patient care is very demanding. It is a lot of energy out with giving care and then add on the extra of running or overseeing a business, your clinic in addition to this. It is not possible to work more than three or four days a week, long term without neglecting your own care. Some doctors work less hours or days a week and some work hard and then take 1 week off every 8-12 weeks in private practice. There are many patterns you can create, but it is essential to take care of yourself if you want to stay practicing and not get burnt out.

If you want to stay in medicine for a long time then you need to take care of yourself. Have you ever gone to a cardiologist and noticed that they look as though they may have a heart attack themselves? Setting your own schedule offers you the freedom to take care of yourself so that you can be a greater help to your patients. This will build a stronger practice as people will see that you look good and know what you are doing.

Clinic patient care ebbs and flows. Some months can be so busy and others dead. Despite this irregularity, it is important to carve out time for yourself.

Exercise

1. Write down anything big or small that you do to recharge and rejuvenate.
2. Think of a time you were significantly stressed by work. Did you recognize the situation or did someone else have to bring it to your attention? What did you do to de-stress? How difficult was it to step away from the stressful situation and engage in self-care?
3. Do you think you are capable of recognizing stress in your life that you have difficulty processing? Can you think of ways that you identify stress now, or ways that you might use?

How do you deal with criticism?

In a private practice you cannot hide behind the large entity of a hospital. When support staff are unhappy in a private practice it reflects directly on you, the owner. Are you prepared to deal with that pressure? When patients are unhappy, or they leave your practice, you will know about it.

When patients are unhappy in a private practice, they will let you know. Suddenly you are in charge of matters related to customer service and personnel management, and most of the issues that arise in those topics begin with complaints, not praise. Sometimes that criticism is entirely fair and useful for you to know. Other times it's a matter of judgment and taste. And many times the patient's complaint is just plain wrong, based on their own misunderstanding, lack of knowledge, or even willful desire to cause trouble or get something for free.

How will you deal with this? Are you capable of dealing with these issues patiently, and without escalating them into unnecessary conflict that can cost you in terms of money and reputation? Are you prepared to deal with regulatory agencies when the matter requires it? Such issues can drag on for months. How well can you live with the uncertainty this brings?

Exercise

1. Think about a time that a patient was dissatisfied with your care. How would you handle the situation knowing that you could not share the burden with a hospital or higher-up?
2. Are you a glass is half empty or glass is half full person?
3. How do you deal with criticism? Be specific. Think of times you were criticized and what you did to fix the problem for yourself and for the other person – or if there was a real problem at all.
4. How do you deal with conflict? Do you try to avoid conflict? Again, think of a case where you were engaged in a conflict over a matter, personal or professional, in the work environment. What was the outcome? Were you satisfied with it? Was the other person? What did you do? What would you do differently?

Questions About Day-to-Day Practice

Where do you go for input on your medical decisions?

In every practice, whether in a hospital or on your own, there are times you want to run something by another provider. There are always new treatments or approaches to health concerns. Keeping up is part of your job, but you can't know everything. Just as important, and often just as confusing, some medical decisions have more than one right answer, often more than one best answer.

One doctor cannot know it all. When you have a practice with a colleague, their different interests and knowledge are useful to have around. They can help optimize the health of your patients and help grow your own skills. Are you connected with other practitioners who will fill this role for you when needed?

1. Write down the names of colleagues you call now when you need to talk over a case. Are these people you work with right now? If so, would they welcome your inquiries if you no longer worked together? If you were in your own practice would you be in competition with them?

2. If the location or situation of your solo practice would cut you off from the colleagues you now call on in this way, are you willing to engage with the medical community where you will be in order to find new colleagues? What might you do to connect with them? How could you offer value to them in exchange for the support you seek?

Would the substance of a patient visit in your own clinic differ from what you have now?

Think about how you interact with patients today. Now think of how you'd like to do it. Is there any difference?

Imagine a patient visit of your own design. You might run more labs than you do, which may be limited to things that rule out the most life-threatening conditions. You would have time to chart completely and even put down a working assessment rather than just the main diagnosis.

Many doctors think of themselves not only as healers and helpers but also as educators. There is rarely any time in a modern-day clinic visit for much education. But if you ran your own clinic, you could make education a priority. You might feel the call of what you learned in medical school, the concept of *docere*, from Cicero, referring to the greater obligation of a teacher. You are able to discuss the whole story of your patients' concerns. The benefits are many. Not only can a deeper doctor-patient relationship enhance outcomes, it can also help prevent physician burnout.

KELLY J. PARCELL, ND

Perhaps you will learn from a patient something that you would not have prescribed but that works for them. Maybe they'll tell you about a new book that touches on your medical interests, or something about fads that has yet to get on the radar of medical professionals. When you're checking the boxes for someone else, a visit can be cramped and limited. If you're the boss, the possibilities are endless.

This can come at a cost, of course. If you accept insurance there are some things that may have to be a part of every visit, and some things you cannot prescribe. If you choose to not accept insurance you regain those freedoms, but you may be doing so at the expense of revenue. Whatever you decide, the priorities that determine the tradeoffs will be yours, and that's latitude that comes only in private practice.

Exercise

1. Can you identify limits on how you currently conduct visits?
2. Do you feel you could give superior care if you could tailor your visits as you see fit?
3. Do you enjoy talking with patients?
4. Do you like to explore a patient's story? What do you do with the information?
5. Are you open to learning new things about medicine from someone who does not have formal credentials?

Do you feel rushed in your time with patients?

What you talk about goes hand in hand with how long you set aside to talk at all.

Maybe you're one of those practitioners who already has a great deal of freedom to spend extended time with a patient. Maybe you have time (or make time) for a personal conversation, letting the interaction go wherever it may. If you're one of those people, count yourself fortunate. There is nothing as fulfilling as building the patient relationship on a true connection built over (literal) time.

But most practitioners feel rushed because they are rushed. They don't skimp on time with patients, but there is definitely pressure to "get to the point" – to find the problem, investigate, diagnosis, and determine or even execute treatment. Many of us feel that if we had more time with those who come to us, we could provide better treatment. We want to know our patients by more than their list of prescriptions.

If you feel rushed... if you feel that you could do a better job probing for underlying causes... if you desire to really hear their story and suspect that you are often reduced to the highlights... if you believe that sometimes just listening provides a kind of healing... if you feel that many patients might come back to you just because you do listen... if this is how you feel, then an integrative practice may be the right choice for you.

Remember when you went to medical school and you had a dream of helping people? You wanted to go into medicine so that you could problem-solve and diagnose and treat not only the disease but also save people's lives. But soon into residency you realized that there was almost no time to connect with patients, what with supervisors breathing down your neck to finish your dozens of charts for the day and to be on time with patient visits. Soon, there was only time to ensure that the critical stuff got covered.

In your own practice, you get to decide how long visits will last. You can get to know patients, learn about their stressors, and learn about their lifestyles. If one answer leads to another question, you can engage.

Exercise

1. Do you feel rushed now? If you feel rushed, is it a major or minor concern?
2. What would you do with extra time for patients? What are some things you might ask?
3. Do you enjoy conversing with patients?
4. Are you good at getting patients to talk when they don't want to talk?

Do insurance coding requirements limit your diagnoses and treatment?

The insurance company wants the patient to get well, of course, but within well-defined limits of time, treatment, and expense. The cold truth is that it is better for the insurance business if many people get a little better than if a few people get a lot better.

One way for you to work around that problem is to open your own practice and stop accepting insurance. This gives you more time to work with patients and more access to a broader range of treatments, but it comes with consequences: you will likely have to see fewer patients to allow time for this (which probably means less income), and that the patients you see will tend to be see more financially comfortable, while patients who are less able to pay for treatment outside of what insurance coverage will go elsewhere.

I hasten to add than none of these consequences is necessarily good or bad. Think of the iron triangle of consulting: you can have it fast, cheap, or good – pick two.

When you have your own practice, how you choose among these options will be up to you. You will have to determine the balance among income, time per patient, flexibility in prescriptions and treatment, and the priority of serving those with a limited ability to pay. The bottom line is this: when you accept insurance, you limit your diagnoses and treatment, and that has an effect on that balance.

If you don't feel constrained by insurance-coding requirements, or those constraints don't bother you, this consideration is unlikely to be a factor in your decision about whether or not to start your own practice. If you feel particularly constrained by insurance-coding requirements, the opportunity to escape them will be appealing. You'll need to think a lot about what you most want to do in terms of community service, self-direction as a practitioner, and income. Remember: to just keep doing it the way you've been doing it is not putting off the decision. It's making a choice in itself.

Exercise

1. Make a list of these three things: income, freedom, service. Write down why each thing matters to you. Now write down a comparison of various combinations: freedom to practice as you see fit versus how much community service I wish to offer. Instead of trying to choose one or the other, write down various situations where the two priorities may come into conflict. What core values are guiding you in thinking about this?

Do your superiors limit your ability to prescribe certain alternative treatments?

Insurance companies impose many limits on how you practice medicine. Your superiors do, too.

Do you feel limited by your superiors? Are you being denied the option of exploring alternatives for your patients, especially those who are not responding to their current medications? Do patients ask for treatments you don't have permission to offer? How do you respond?

For example, perhaps your patient has high cholesterol and is afraid of prescriptions and cardiologists. Are there natural alternatives you want to offer, such as red yeast rice extract, that you're not allowed to choose? Have you ever wanted to do an IV therapy or try an off-label use of a drug that your bosses won't allow? If you have been overruled, how much did this bother you? How much benefit do you think your patient missed?

Also consider this: superiors are sometimes thoughtlessly difficult but most of the time they are protecting you from certain liabilities and problems. Without those bosses, you lose that benefit. Are you willing to accept the exposure that comes with the freedom to step out from behind your superiors?

Exercise

1. How often are you overruled by superiors? Do you accept it and go along, or do you carry that frustration for a long time? How long?
2. Have you ever been overruled and "done it anyway"? How did it work out? Be specific in terms of your attitude, your level of worry, and patient satisfaction.
3. Make a list of the times you wished you could have gone off label and later found out you would have been making a damaging decision. Then make a list of those occasions when going off label worked out well. Finally, make a list of the times you feel failure to go off label cost a patient in significant terms of quality of life. Which of these happened most often? How did you feel about each occurrence? What would you do different, knowing the outcomes as you do now?

Do your visits go beyond immediate problems to address preventative medicine?

As doctors we are trained to begin by identifying immediate, life-threatening issues, then taking action on them. From there we go to things that prompted the visit. We do not often enough get to preventative medicine. As naturopathic practitioners, prevention is a matter near and dear to our hearts. It's often very important to our patients, too.

It ought to be. The opportunity to work on preventative medicine is for many of us one of the great attractions of starting our own practice. We don't have time for it in other settings but if it's your practice, you can choose to make time.

Patients deserve more than a remedy. They deserve to know why they are sick and what they can do to prevent problems in the future. I think of *disease* as *dis-ease*, reflecting disharmony in the body, mind, and spirit. Preventative medicine goes to the heart of that.

If you operate your own practice, you will be able to prioritize preventative medicine – and as usual this will be at the expense of how many patients you can see in a day, which is an indirect way of saying that your income from seeing patients will probably go down a bit. Is this something that is important to you given the drawbacks and advantages? If so, consider it another reason to choose private practice.

Exercise

1. How often do you wish for time to discuss preventative medicine in a visit but lack that time?
2. Do you often think of things you would like to tell a patient about prevention? Do you tell them or hold back? Why?
3. How much of an improvement do you think most patients would see if you gave them more on preventative medicine?
4. If you could spend more time on preventative medicine, what services and products might you offer that could make up financially for the decline in patients seen per day? Be specific.

Are you intimidated by patients who seem to know more than you do?

The rise of the Internet means patients know more than ever about health and treatment. This can be valuable when what they know is accurate. It's also a good indicator of someone who cares about their own well-being, and it often means they will be better than other patients at adhering to your advice. Some things they come in with will be pure misinformation, of course, often dangerous if acted on. But most of what they bring in will be true in some sense but not very useful without context and experience.

How do you feel when patients come in with a great deal of information to sort through? Do you have a way you always handle them? Do you dismiss them? Hear them out? Encourage them?

Sometimes you will not have any idea about the remedy they have found. You will lose the patient if you minimize their questions. You will gain trust if you align with the patient and let them know you want to spend time researching the question and leave them with no answer for that visit. Are you comfortable with that?

Humility is an important trait as a doctor in private practice. Sometimes it feels like we get out of school knowing only three things: the basic operation of the body, foundational treatments, and how to avoid making somebody worse than when they came in. It's better than that, of course, but the feeling of being overwhelmed is a standard feature of the early days of an independent practice. Can you find the self-confidence to deal with that?

1. When a patient tells you something that you did not know, what is your first reaction? Do you say that you already know it even when you don't? Do you offer to do research, and do you actually do that research and follow up?
2. How do you disabuse a patient of believing something they are convinced is true?
3. How do you react when a patient tells you that you are wrong when you know you are correct?

Questions About Business
Skill and Finances

How comfortable are you with the risk of being on your own?

When you are on your own, you have only your malpractice insurance to protect you. Patients have direct contact with you in the sense that your decision constitutes the final word on matters relating to both their treatment and their business relationship with the practice. There's no administrator you can defer to, no "that's out of my hands" refuge you can claim. I've asked you to think about this in terms of your medical decisions. Now think about it in terms of business.

Are you willing to let go of the safety of a hospital or clinic for legal protection and oversight?

Are you prepared to address reputational matters in social media?

Are you willing to deal with disputes about quality of service and adjustments in payment due?

Have you considered how you would react to complaints filed with a state board or professional association? Have you considered how you would manage the time such complaints may consume?

Have you considered the loss of income that might come from a suspension of your practice during certain types of professional investigations, and how malpractice insurance can ameliorate the loss?

There are risks to prepare for – but preparing for them doesn't mean the worst things will definitely occur. An independent practice is usually home to good care and great relationships with patients. In reality, patients rarely take dramatic action against doctors with integrity, honesty, and good bedside manner – candor and caring go a long way. A compassionate staff helps a lot, too, and since you do the hiring and firing you can make sure your staff reflects the attitudes you demand of yourself.

Exercise

1. Have you had experience in business? What was it like personally and professionally? Would you consider the episode to have been successful? In what ways? Be specific.
2. Have you taken courses in accounting, bookkeeping, or business? Have you learned any of those skills independently? Do you think you could benefit from taking such courses, either formally or by studying books? Are you willing to do so?
3. Do money issues arise frequently and give you stress, or do you avoid them by planning financial matters in advance? If you are not currently engaged in planning your finances, are you willing to start doing so?

How do you feel about "doing without" and the uncertainty of starting a business?

Starting a practice from scratch is a leap of faith. It's like jumping out of a plane for the first time after weeks of sky-diving training. It's scary as hell and you have to trust in your preparation. When you decide to go for it, you will almost certainly soar. But once you jump you'll spend some scary moments falling through the air, waiting for the chute to open. For a while, you're at the mercy of forces you have planned for but that are out of your control.

For my husband and me, it took about two years until we were in a financially sound situation – consistently in the black. That's a reasonable amount of "in-between" time you should assume, too, in between opening your doors and seeing your practice become financially sustainable. You have to be comfortable with knowing that for the first two years you will be living with financial uncertainty. If you don't have a loan or savings to start up your business and fill the income gaps during that in-between time, you will have to use credit cards, a line of credit, investors, spousal support, or a second mortgage to help.

The less money you have to start, the more work you will have to do on your own. For some practitioners this is more than they are willing to take on. For others, it's interesting and occasionally fun: they get to work on aspects of business they never got to do before.

We started NatureMed by simply renting an office space and ordering supplements, IV supplies, and about 30 patient charts. We used credit cards for everything and were in the red for about two years. We had no receptionist and when a job needed doing, we were the ones who did it.

Whether you enjoy the challenge or dread it, these sorts of challenges will be a part of your experience. Consider whether you want to accept it, because there will be no getting around it.

I was prepared for the experience more than most because I was raised without much money in the house. My mother had only an 8th grade education and therefore worked low-wage jobs. We used food stamps, bought our clothes at thrift stores, and did our laundry at the laundromat. At one point my mother was so desperate for a house instead of a rented few rooms that she moved us out into the wilderness, 25 miles from school, to serve as caretaker for a house that had only cold water and no toilet or electricity.

Talk about doing without. We lived there for one year when I was a sophomore in high school. After that experience I learned that I could "do without" a lot, and for a long time.

The first couple years of a new practice is a time when you are going to do without, perhaps for the first time. Some of the things you now consider to be necessities may become luxuries. Before you proceed, consider your level of comfort with that.

Exercise

1. What do you do with deferred gratification?
2. Have you had problems in the past with debt?
3. Do you feel resentful when you have to wait for things? If you do, how does that feeling manifest itself?
4. Are you truly willing to "do without" for two or more years on the hope – not the guarantee, but the hope – that you will have the things you want after it passes?

Do you have money up front to start your own practice?

Before you have income, you'll have expenses: rent, equipment, inventory, business services, taxes, licenses, salaries (including your own), marketing, and construction and maintenance of a website and an online presence. You may end up spending a great deal of money, and it can easily run into the six-figure range, depending on your location and how expansive your practice will be.

Do you have personal resources? Family resources? Can you secure a business loan, and are you willing to incur such debt? Do you have friends or family who can lend you money?

Exercise

1. Make a line-by-line budget sheet. Be sure you've included everything, that you have built in unanticipated costs. How much will you need to spend, month by month, for the first two years? How much can you anticipate in revenue? How much does it offset what you will need? Run it by other people whom you trust, and who know about medical practices, business, or both.

2. If you do not have enough personal resources to operate without any outside funding (don't worry, most people can't), find out if you qualify for small-business loans from banks and from the government. Shop around for repayment terms. Consider length of the repayment term, the interest rate, and penalties if any for early payoff.

Simple Budget Sheet

All Expenses	Jan	Feb	Mar	Apr
Salary				
Malpractice Insurance				
EHR				
Rent				
Postage				
Supplies				
Total				
Income				
Are you over or under?				

Are you willing to spend a part of your time doing marketing?

Patients aren't just going to appear at your door, of course. You'll have to make a coordinated and heavy public effort to let them know you are open for business, and to attract them to what you provide. How will you do that?

Are you willing to give free lectures? Are you willing to do the research to find or create opportunities for those lectures?

Are you willing to network and meet with other providers?

Are you willing to cold call other providers to introduce yourself in the first place?

Have you thought about how you will advertise – and if you will advertise? Would you hire someone to do a promotion for you, and can you afford to do so? Can you afford not to?

Are you comfortable having to be the one who brings in business? If not, could you do it anyway? Could you afford to pay someone else to do the job?

1. Call newspapers and do online searches to find out how much local public relations services are and what the cost and type of advertising options are in your area. Meet with sellers of advertising to learn how precisely they can target types of audiences and what their viewing rates are (meaning how often people tend to see certain types of ads when they are placed a particular number of times) and what the conversion rates tend to be (meaning how often the viewing of an ad leads to a call, email, or other conversion to revenue or potential revenue).

2. Do a calculation of how much you would have to spend in order to get conversions worth various amounts. A casual calculation is fine.

Review your answers.

If you've answered everything – really written down something after every query – good. It's important that you do that. If you didn't write something down for every question, go back and do that before you proceed.

It's important that you do more than "think about it." It's easy to feel positive or negative about something, but examining the details can either reinforce that good feeling or show you where you've been kidding yourself. Writing things down forces you to identify and consider those details. How does it do that? You can't write down a feeling. You can write down things. Think of a patient who says she feels bad and that she's feeling "achy." You don't just write a prescription to fix "achy" and send her on her way. You find out exactly what's going on: you ask where it hurts, what the pain is like, and when the pain occurs. You take a history. You order labs. You get the specifics.

Then you write them down. Because how you feel is one thing, but what the data indicate can show that the feeling is right, misleading, or completely wrong.

Review your responses to this section. Look at the numbers and the facts. Consider the challenges and your attitude toward them. Think about your interest in or capacity to accept those challenges that you don't care to engage in. And think about the pleasure and pride of your own practice as the payoff to meeting those challenges.

Consider that effort as the barrier to entry. Everything has a barrier to entry, from getting into college to qualifying for the Olympics. Some people decide that trying to overcome the barrier is worth it. Others set their sights elsewhere.

There's no right or wrong conclusion. What you decide is right for you – that's the correct answer.

Spend some time thinking about it. Spend some time talking to people you love and people you trust. Write out your thoughts. Then, in a few days, write down one of these sentences. Write it at the bottom of this page:

I am going to start my own practice.
For now, I am not going to start my own practice.

Then stick with your decision. If it's a no but you're not sure, wait at least three months before re-considering. If you don't set a time like that, a delay during which you live with your decision, you won't be able to move on to other things, and that's not going to be productive.

If it's a yes, proceed to the next section and start the work of launching your practice.

It's your decision, but I'll offer only one bit of personal opinion. If you're on the fence, do it. As a doctor you are naturally cautious. Entrepreneurism can be a little scary for people like us. But if you feel positive about this opportunity, chances are you're just waiting for a sort-of sign that this is the path to take. Here's your sign.

PART II: How to Find the Best Place for You to Practice

In this section, we'll go through research and personal decision-making to find where you might practice to be both successful and happy.

Kelly's Experience

I always knew that I wanted to return to my hometown of Boulder, Colorado after medical school. I wanted to live there and I wanted to practice there. It just made sense. Connections and community were strong there, plus I would have a pool of people with whom I could begin to grow a practice.

But what you would like to do, what you are able to do, and what is wise to do are sometimes very different things. Choosing the right place to live and to practice requires serious consideration of all three paths.

When I went into medical school, I was single. When I graduated I was engaged. When I finished residency, I was married and about to become a mother. I now had to negotiate where to set up practice with another person as well as think about the challenges of raising a child, childcare and family life!

As graduation approached for my husband, Steve, we began to think about where we would like to live and practice, where we could practice, and where it be wise to practice. Steve shares my adventurous spirit and we were set on success together, but even armed with his undergraduate minor in business he didn't know much more than I did about the practical considerations of independent practice. Still, he consulted with someone for a little basic advice and we started to work together on our plan for a clinic.

Step one was choosing a location. It was challenging but it also showed us one of the unspoken benefits of starting your own practice: you get to make yourself fully aware of what you really want in life, and where you truly wish to be. We thought about what we wanted, where we would like to be in a few years, and what makes us happy, satisfied, and fulfilled. We made a list, a real list on paper, and we did not allow ourselves to make this decision the easy way, with casual conversations and no research. Our list was specific, addressing issues of quality of life for ourselves and our children, the size and nature of the competition, what we could afford to spend and how much that would buy in terms of housing and resources in any given area, access to childcare, and our own scope of practice as naturopathic doctors. Hanging over the whole things was the fact that we had little money.

We were going to have a child, so we thought being near family would be good. His mother was in Connecticut, a state where licensure allows wider scope of practice for NDs. My family and his sister were living in Boulder, where Colorado rules were far more limiting.

After much deliberation and research, we decided that Boulder gave us more reasons to move there than Connecticut even though our scope of practice would be limited.

The questions we worked through are compiled and expanded upon in this part of the book.

As you read, you will go through the process we went through in our own lives, question by question and step by step. As you think about this question of where to live and practice, I encourage you to throw off limits, and to quit worrying about the expectations of other people – or earlier versions of yourself. Think seriously about what you want in life, where you can get it, and your willingness to compromise on some things in order to get other things. The decision we made was rewarding, but making the decision was rewarding as well. It can be the same for you.

How to Use This Section

If you've decided to open a practice, congratulations. This part will help you begin thinking about where you would like to practice.

If you're still exploring whether this is the right move for you (and you're still reading), that's okay, too. It may help you make your decision to think about where you might wish to practice.

In this short section, I'll describe things to consider as you decide where to locate a practice. It's a matter of finding the right balance: you'll think about what you want personally and professionally in a location, and how closely any given region can meet those needs.

You'll find that this decision is best made when you categorize your interests. There are things you would like to have, and others you must have. Some things will require you to rank personal priorities. For instance, you might like to be near the mountains so you can ski in your off time. Is this a thing you would like, or is it a necessity? Other things are matters of law and regulation. You might wish to supply a certain kind of treatment that you can provide only in certain states. Is this a thing that you have to have to practice your approach to medicine, or is it something you could do without?

Spend some time thinking about your interests, your priorities, and the matters on which you will not compromise. The more detail you bring to this process, the easier it can be.

Find a place you love.

Do you love New York City? Are you most comfortable in the wide-open spaces of the west? Do you find a New England winter the sort of thing that feels romantic even in the coldest months? Begin by thinking about where you want to live in terms of the affection you have for the region. Do you love it there? Could you love it there?

Love is hard to define, maybe impossible. But think about which places make you feel special, which places you can take or leave, and which you just can't stand. Think too about what you'll love in the future, and what you might come to love as circumstances change. Do you intend to marry? Date? Have children? Do you see yourself as single for life?

Does the way of life in a given place bring you satisfaction or even joy? Is it full of people you'd like to be around? In most ways people are the same wherever you go, but culture varies from place to place. Mississippi and Minnesota, for instance, are both filled with nice people but the way they go about their days can be quite different. Also consider that we often think of stereotypes instead of reality. When I mention Huntsville, Alabama, your mind may go to a Southern stereotype that begins and ends with pickup trucks, rifle racks, and Lynyrd Skynyrd songs. Yet Huntsville, Alabama is home to much of

America's space program, and has one of the highest densities of PhDs per square mile of any area in the United States. So don't assume things about a region. Go there. Find out.

Loving where you live matters, because you're probably going to be there a while. The economic efficiencies of a practice come in the long term. You will likely want to stay in the same town or region for 10 to 20 years. For most of us, practice takes at least a couple years just to become profitable, and steady success comes only with sustained presence and effort over many years. Starting over somewhere else means leaving behind your investment in people and reputation.

Wherever you choose, be sure it's a place that you love, or at least a place you can fall in love with.

Consider whether the place you choose meets your personal needs.

Ask yourself if the area supports your personal interests and lifestyle.

Think about your interests and passions other than medicine. Maybe your passion outside of work is, for instance, some kind of art. Does this area support the arts, especially in terms of an independent community of artists and lovers of art? Are they "doing" your art, such as popular music, painting, sculpting, improv, or theater?

Does your religious or spiritual practice require a community of people who feel the same way, and who meet regularly? Not every religion is well established in every area. Check into this, if it's important to you.

My husband and I love the outdoors, and we are athletes. We are big on cycling, skiing, and nature. We wouldn't want to live in a place where we couldn't do them. For us, finding a place that supports this was a primary concern, not just something that would be nice to have.

We also insisted that wherever we chose to live had to satisfy us in terms of our children's interests and potential interests. It had to make us feel safe for them, too. And it needed to be close to as much of our extended family as possible, because spending time with them is a priority for us.

If loving a place is about the intangible part of attraction, finding a place that supports your interests is a question you can answer with a few phone calls and Google searches. Do them.

Find out if the population you want to serve is present.

It takes about 2000 citizens to support a practice. What is the population of the area and is there a place for you?

What is the demographic of the area you want to practice? Are these the people you are best equipped to serve, or whom you would like to serve? Do you have something unique to offer them?

Are people open to natural medicine/alternative medicine? Is there a community of people already interested?

What is the average income? What about how they pay for healthcare: is it a community of government workers who rely exclusively on insurance, or are they able to pay cash for services? This factors into your practice, since you will have to decide if you're going to be a cash practice or an insurance practice.

What seem to be common health issues for the area? For instance, many states and counties (by some measures, most of them!) have significant populations dealing with obesity. If you practice in such a place, that's going to be a part of what you encounter, regardless of what else a patient presents. Is the kind of medicine a given area most often needs the kind of medicine you want to practice? In this case, would you be happy to spend a significant part of your day doing weight-loss medicine?

My best friend opened her practice in a town she loved (checked that box!) whose characteristics lined up well with her lifestyle (checked the second box, too). But she had not thought about the financial characteristics of patients there. She wanted to have a cash practice, but it didn't work out that way: about 90% of her billing was insurance based. It was a "government town" and everyone wanted to use their insurance, which was quite a good deal for them even if it wasn't the best arrangement for the practitioner. The bottom line came clear quickly: if she did not take insurance, patients would go to other doctors who did. Thus my friend was forced into a practice that was largely insurance based, which was not at all what she had in mind.

Get to know your competition.

Do an Internet search for doctors in the area where you would like to practice. Investigate their websites. Read their reviews. Consider how you fit in. Would you be providing treatments not currently available? Do you bring a significantly different attitude about natural medicine? Is there anything that separates you from the competition? If so, identify what it is so you can make use of the difference. If not, consider what might make you stand out from the crowd.

Try to meet with providers in the area for advice. Some may turn you down, but it's almost always the case that a few will be pleased to help a fellow practitioner. Ask them what they did to get their practices going. Ask them how long they've been there. Get to know them and see what you can learn – and make a colleague and friend out of your competitor.

Finally, don't let the presence of competition dissuade you. Competition is good: it makes for better practitioners and more discerning patients. Consider opening a practice close to a busy hospital or the busy part of town. See how your services, such as an IV clinic, might fare next to a gym, for instance. As my father used to say, "If you are in the shoe business and you want to grow, set up next to Nike."

PART III: How to Prepare to Open Your Practice

In this section, you'll go through the things that have to be done before opening day.

Kelly's Experience

Do as much as you can *before* your doors open.

In this section I identify the basics and more, such as naming your practice, getting a website, securing a logo, writing a mission statement, planning the extent and nature of your practice, setting up back-office functions (meaning financial and management structures), hiring staff, and securing the best physical location for your office. In other words, this section tells you how to "set the table" before you call everybody to dinner.

To keep it all from feeling overwhelming, create a calendar with items to do on each day of your week. Don't make the common mistake of just writing up a "to do" list, doing as much as you can each day, then adding to it as new things come up. Your list will only get longer, and you'll quickly start feeling as if you're not making progress – because your "to do" list is never getting any shorter.

By scheduling your work on a calendar, you'll see at the end of each day that you've done things that need to be done, and that you are closer to doing the things that need to be done to allow you to launch. It is the act of completing the daily list itself, each day, that gives you a sense of momentum, and that momentum is vital for getting through the setup with a healthy attitude. Can you do more on some days or even every day? Of course! But now that extra work will truly feel like a bonus achievement each day, and not just more slogging toward a goal post that seems to keep moving further into the future.

As you plan for opening, keep in mind the image you want to project, because it's influential. A clear and compelling image is conveyed in the way you execute the dozens of things that will be a part of your launch. Present an image of your practice that suggests confidence and reliability – think of your practice as bigger than it is and act like that's the case. If you're a competent physician, the "steak" is already taken care of. Think also about the "sizzle." Make your images slick, your website professional. Perception is reality.

Opening your own integrative practice is really satisfying. Of course, that good feeling doesn't come without stress and hard work, but it's manageable. And nothing great ever comes without effort. That was our experience. We learned as we were going along. I hope our experience can cut down on your expense of time and worry as you make your own way through this process.

How to Use This Section

Consider the steps here as a way to further determine your commitment to the work of starting a practice. You may discover that there's more to this than you thought, more than you're willing to do, or that it requires more resources than you are willing or able to assemble just now.

Then again, you may find that it's easier than you expected.

Whatever you find, it's valuable because the activities here are pushing you toward a decision you can have confidence in. Each step you explore will give you clarity about whether or not you wish to take the next step. You don't have to know it all right now. You don't have to do it all right now, either.

Here you'll find categories of actions you'll need to take. Under each category I've listed a series of things you'll need to do. To make good use of this section, read it thoroughly, make notes at the end, and make a day-and-date plan for doing every action you find here. If it's hiring an office manager, make a plan for where you'll place ads and conduct interviews. If it's setting up banking, choose a day to go to the bank of your choice and set up the accounts you need.

A lot of times you're going to feel as if you're not yet ready, that you don't yet know enough, or that you need to consider more options. Don't listen to that voice. Move ahead anyway. It will be easier to fix something you've done partially incorrectly than to wait until you know everything.

If you wait until you're "ready," you'll never begin. Get started. Turn the page!

Action Item: Define the Scope of Your Practice

Decide what your practice will include beyond patient visits.

You won't make your entire income by patient visits alone, nor should you try to.

You'll need other ways to grow your revenue base and to preserve your time for other profitable or interesting activities. Think about what kinds of services can be administered by someone other than you, someone who bills at a lower hourly rate than you can bill. Anyone who does work on your behalf but at a lower wage is making money for you and for your clinic.

Take a look at this list of just a few things you might offer in your practice that will directly create revenue or restore time lost in activities that other staff besides you can do. You're going to need this kind of thing. Consider your interest in these choices and willingness to do them. Consider other ideas you may have seen in other practices, too.

- You may want to sell supplements and nutraceuticals. While MDs are taught to perceive this as a conflict of interest, naturopathic doctors understand that these offerings add value. Some over-the-counter vitamins, supplements, and nutraceuticals are of dubious quality and efficacy. Since we are better equipped than patients to judge these products in terms of quality, safety, and efficacy, we can offer superior choices, saving them time and potential trouble, and giving them greater confidence in their treatment. (I'll write more about this below.)

- Look into a concierge-style "lane," common among MDs and DOs. This is a "membership" approach that allows patients to visit as many times as they wish per month or year, within limits you define. The additional profit comes from patients who use fewer visits than they could have purchased with the same amount of money, and superior outcomes are more likely given the typically higher interest in adherence seen among patients serious enough to invest in their health this way. Concierge service also provides savings on prospecting for new patients. The downside is that some months may be considerably busier than others. Also, you'll need support staff to monitor patients' use of the service to keep prices and limits in sync with yours goals for profitability and occupation of your time.

- Consider offering bloodwork and other labs. It is convenient for you and your patients to be able to do inhouse blood draws. Some expenses are, surprisingly, already covered for you. State labs usually provide free accounts for the use of centrifuge time, and provide consumable supplies such as butterflies, straight needles, tourniquets, and tubes. You can charge for the service, of course, enjoy service on your schedule, and see to it that labs get done correctly and to your standards.

- If it's permitted in your area and allowed by association guidelines, consider offering IV therapy. It's not as simple to set up as most other offerings, but it can be highly profitable even with the investment. You'll need a clean room, a hood, an account with a compounding pharmacy, a refrigerator, catheter-use training for nurses or EMTs who work for you, an emergency protocol kit, on-site oxygen, and several other things. You'll also need space, typically a dedicated room with recliners and IV stands, plus a staff member who monitors or even administers treatment.

- Consider offering procedures such as pellet therapy, certain gynecological examinations, and minor surgical procedures. Investigate what you'll need to do with them in terms of things such as a room with a sink and a counter, appropriate exam tables, instruments such as trocars, and an autoclave.

- You can offer acupuncture services. You'll need a practitioner, of course, and a room for visits. In this way you expand clinic offerings while taking your profit largely by functioning as the practitioner's "agent" and landlord. Offering massage comes with the same benefits and obligations.

- Some clinics offer hyperbaric oxygen treatments (HBOT), saunas, whirlpools, and other device-based treatments that require relatively significant investment in hardware before you see profit from using them. They can of course be both helpful and profitable. If you don't launch your clinic with these already in place but want to consider having them in the future, be sure you plan for the space, plumbing, electrical requirements, regulatory requirements, and separate rooms you will need. There's nothing worse than running out of space a couple years after you launch, especially when you could have easily planned for it up front.

Have you seen other practitioners doing things in this additional-profit realm that appealed to you? Are they things you already know how to do, things you could learn, or things you could figure out on your own? Do you have ideas for offerings that you haven't seen anywhere else – unique services and treatments that might set your practice apart?

How much of your practice would you prefer to see dedicated to these sorts of thing? Think in terms of hours per day or week, dollars or percentage of income, and your own priority for how you would like to spend your time versus how much additional income you need from these offerings.

Beyond adding offerings like these, you can save time and money by preparing handouts patients can take with them describing details of common remedies and treatments. It increases adherence and can reduce your having to re-explain some things down the road. In that vein, consider having a staff member meet with patients after your visit to review all that they have been instructed to do. It will enhance adherence as well and raise your reputation as an engaged practitioner who really cares about patients. If you are providing some of those other services, this also provides an opportunity to offer them to patients in a setting where they won't be rushed hearing about them.

Decide the size and scope of any in-house pharmacy you wish to provide.

Many clinics provide an in-house pharmacy for convenience of patients and providers as well as for an additional stream of income. Consider what you would want to sell. Among the most common offerings are nutrients that you will use as alternatives to prescription drugs. Think of the main areas you want to focus and be sure that the key nutrients are in your clinic pharmacy. Some of these supplements and nutraceuticals include

- Cholesterol management alternatives,
- Multi-vitamins,
- Vitamin D, C, and activated B complex,
- CoQ10 and fish oil, and
- Remedies for adrenal health and sleep, bone density and the GI tract.

You don't have to stock anything if you don't want to. Nearly every wholesaler offers an online feature that allows you as a naturopath to register with them. When your patients log on to the site and enter a code you've provided, they receive a discount, and you get a portion of the revenue from every sale. (And they keep track of it for you, too.)

If you want to carry a small inventory in house, consider stocking "designer" nutrients that are not particularly common, and let patients purchase their more ordinary needs (e.g., Vitamin C, Vitamin A, zinc, etc.) online or at a health food or grocery store.

The next step in expanding your pharmacy might be to stock more items. Beyond that, though, consider establishing a "private label" brand. This is just taking a standard product from a wholesaler and paying them a small fee to label the bottle with your name or the name of your clinic or brand. If you go this route you'll typically have to buy in bulk and store it (and sell the stock before it expires), so there is more expense and risk this way. But if you are seeing consistent sales of particular products, the advantages include the addition to your portfolio of direct advertising. That labeled bottle with your name on it will sit on your patients' kitchen counter. When their friends come, they'll see the company name, and see it associated with a high-quality naturopathic product. You passively solicit business and enhance your reputation.

Finally, note that you might find some ideas and opportunities in the graduation fair typically held after graduation from naturopathic school. Labs and supplement companies set up booths to inform new graduates (and, if they're allowed in, practitioners who are already in the field) on their products and services. These representatives will set up accounts on the spot and take orders. If you attend one of these events, collect contact cards, wholesale price lists, and catalogs. If you are still planning your in-house pharmacy and are not yet ready to order, ask for an extension of a year for opening orders and any discounts or benefits they provide with new accounts. Companies will usually grant the extension in the hope of having you around for a long time.

Action Item: Formalize Your Identity as a Practice

Compose a mission
statement.

A mission statement formalizes for the public and for you the philosophy and purpose of your practice. It states what your goals are and, often, which communities are your focus of service. It should be detailed but clear – and relatively brief, 60 words or less. Some clinics have long mission statements, complete with sections about principles, vision, and other categories. You can write such a thing if you want, but a shorter mission statement is actually more powerful because it forces you to identify the "bones" of your practice and to clearly state what you want for your patients and for yourself.

Here is what we use on our website. You'll notice we don't call it a mission statement. Instead, we label is plainly as our philosophy and the thing that makes us unique – plain language that I believe makes our clinic more friendly and accessible:

Our naturopathic philosophy:

Every person and condition is unique, and we work with you to develop a personalized treatment plan that will offer the greatest benefit. By addressing the underlying cause of disease, we can optimize health, extend your "health span" and help you avert expensive medical procedures and illnesses. Your benefit is disease prevention and peace of mind. We will spend the time it takes to answer all your questions and develop a detailed, long-term treatment plan that addresses all of your health concerns.

What makes us unique?

We "bridge the gap" between conventional and alternative medicine. We are the experts in naturopathic, alternative, complementary, integrative and holistic medicine. This training and experience allows us to provide the best of both worlds. We offer prescriptions as well as nutritional and herbal therapies to achieve results. We work together in the clinic as a team to provide comprehensive care as well as an openness to work with you off site medical doctor to ensure continuity of care.

Choose a name.

Now that you've spent time thinking about why you're in practice, it's time to think about a way to quickly evoke that idea. In short, what is the name of your clinic going to be?

The name sets the tone for what you're going to do. At the least it tells people how to find you – what your name is in the marketplace. At the most it tells people who you are, what you do, and what you stand for.

That sounds like a big task, but it doesn't have to be. Your name can be as meaningful or as prosaic as you wish. This is one of those points in the process where it all depends on how much value you intend to mine from a name.

I say think about it. Try out a few names with friends, family, and colleagues. If you have patients from your current setup, see what some of them might think. If you find something that you feel passionately about, go with it. But if you come up cold, there's nothing wrong with using something simple and generic.

(You can always use your name but if you intend to bring on partners, you'll have to revisit the issue at that time.)

Write a tagline.

Your tagline is your mission statement in a phrase. It's great to have a tagline for marketing and advertising. It tells people right away what you do and who you are. A tagline ought to be no more than a few words. Here are some examples:

- *We believe in nature. And we believe in you.*
- *Helping you live your best life.*
- *A place of harmony and health.*
- *The home of the natural approach.*
- *Let's get better together.*
- *A sanctuary for better living.*
- *Nature is at the center of everything we do.*
- *Here for you. Here for life.*

The tagline that's best for you will probably come from experimenting with words, checking out other taglines you like (even those from businesses that are unrelated to naturopathy), and bouncing around ideas in spare moments. It can be fun to come up with a tagline. It doesn't have to give you an "a ha!" moment. It just has to be accurate, evocative, and encouraging – and it has to feel right to you.

Get a logo.

At its best, a logo is a visual representation of your clinic or your mission statement and tagline.

I suggest hiring a graphic designer to come up with the logo, and to then produce it in the various electronic formats you'll need for printed and online use on bills, stationery, ads, promotional/information material, and of course your website and social media posts. Even if you're computer savvy, you may be unfamiliar with the many different formats and resolutions that various applications require. If you prefer to avoid the expense of a designer, you can build something yourself, though you'll need some expertise. There are also many automated online services that create logos based on your input. Their work product often looks a little "canned" but it's professional, and using their services is an easy way to save money.

Many doctors in the field of natural medicine will use natural images for their logos, such as images of healing plants. We started out with the image of Silybum (milk thistle) which is an important medicinal plant in alternative medicine for the liver. Since liver function is a cornerstone of health, we chose this powerful plant image for our logo.

A year later, our clinic had grown so we decided to hire a graphic designer to re-create our materials and move us toward a more polished presentation. After a few meetings and many ideas, we settled on what we have today: two overlapping leaves with a space in between. This represents our tagline and the core value of our practice: "bridging the gap between conventional and alternative medicine."

Explore whether you need a trademark.

If you are using your own name, it is exceedingly rare to need to trademark or to copyright it. It may not even be possible. (Some exceptions may occur if you practice under a variation of your name. For instance, if your name is Ellis and you practice under a non-obvious variation such as "Big Doc Elly" there may be an issue of protecting the mark. See your attorney.)

However, if you are using a name that is catchy and common or that can be used across industries of similar interests, a trademark can be important. For instance, when we named our clinic there was no business in the area with our name. However, with the boom of the legal marijuana industry, soon we saw that these companies were using the words *natural* and *medicine* in their titles. We decided to trademark the name after we found that there was a medical marijuana company with the same name as ours in a neighboring town.

Finally, there is a little-known but thriving industry in business-name extortion. Sometimes an individual of low character will attempt to make a quick buck by casting about for unusual names that are not formally owned by their primary user.

This "legal extortionist" will file appropriate papers to make their claim official, then do the minimum amount the law requires to shift their status from "squatter" to a recognized entity. The last step? Sue the original owner for infringement. This leaves you with an expensive choice: abandon a name whose reputation you have built, spend a literal fortune fighting a claim you may not even win, or settle by paying what amounts to ransom, which is what the little bastard had in mind all along.

I learned about trademarking from my father's business experience. When a business gets big enough and has a presence, there is name recognition. Smaller companies can grow recognition by having similar words or spelling or a company in a different industry can use that same name and gain traffic or recognition through name searches. There's nothing wrong with that. But when someone uses it for extortion, they've crossed a line. Plan for it because when it happens, it'll be too late to do much except write a check and grit your teeth.

Action Item: Establish Yourself in the Professional Community

Become a member of your state association and meet with the board.

Create relationships. Contact the state association and let them know you are coming. Get involved. Meet other doctors. Collegiality is valuable and enjoyable. It can also be the source of important opportunities.

Within a week of moving back to Colorado, Steve and I attended our annual state association meeting. We met all of the other naturopathic doctors in the state. As we went around the room introducing ourselves, I mentioned we had just moved in and were starting our practice. Over lunch a woman came up to me and asked me if I would be willing to cover for her during her maternity. That connection was the beginning of building my own practice.

Formally connect with those who set the standards that apply to you.

If you're a naturopathic doctor, learn the limitations on your scope of practice in the state where you intend to practice. If you're an MD or a DO, find out what your state medical board's "hot topics" are, especially in terms of regulatory concerns. This is important as you begin to think about the type of therapies you want to provide. At the time of this writing, it is my sense that some of their main concerns are

- IV therapy,
- Non-surgical weight loss strategies,
- Integrative oncology,
- Ultraviolet blood irradiation or light therapy,
- BHRT (bioidentical hormone replacement therapy), and
- Alternatives to prescription drugs.

The focus of regulation will vary from state to state, depending on the priorities of elected officials, practicing doctors, and consumer groups. For instance, you state medical board may not approve of IV chelation therapy or off-label drug use, while the next state over may have rules that are the opposite. When we moved to Colorado to practice, we knew we were coming to a state where, at the time, naturopathic doctors were almost completely unregulated. Our passion was to practice as we were trained, and to do whatever it took to help people get healthy. We felt strongly about providing IV therapy and using prescription drugs when indicated, along with more natural versions of conventional medications such as desiccated thyroid or BHRT. That left us with three options: hire a medical doctor to fill the gap in scope of practice, try to get the law changed, or go practice somewhere other than Colorado.

We got the law changed! We could not have done it if we hadn't made connections with those who make and enforce the regulations. State rules govern literally everything you do. Get connected and stay connected to the people who make the decisions.

Action Item: Establish the Practice as a Business

Set up accounting, bookkeeping, tax planning, and banking.

Bookkeeping is the day-to-day record keeping of all your business transactions and purchases. Think of it as keeping track of your checkbook and savings account.

Accounting is a little more involved. It is taking a subjective look at income and outflow and imposing a professional judgment on what that means for the business. Bookkeepers, by contrast, keep track of what you spend and take in without much concern for what the implications may be. Accountants are legally certified to do more. In particular, they advise you on what your financial situation means for your long- and short-term goals, and even viability, in light of what is legal and customary. Sometimes a professional accountant offers bookkeeping services, meaning they take in the data and analyze it as well, but a bookkeeper is not credentialed to make the decisions of an accountant.

These services can come in the form of a financial services practice, a single individual (an accountant who offers bookkeeping and tax planning, too), or several independent professionals. Just be sure to secure these services. In our experience, the bigger your clinic and the more employees you have, the more important it becomes to have the accountant and book-keeper in one company.

Work with your accountant and bookkeeper (if they're not the same person or firm) to set up banking. You can do it yourself, but these support people may have relationships in place that they can leverage for you to make banking easier and less expensive. Secure company credit cards and checks as well, choose who can use the cards or sign the checks, and set a dollar-limit above which an expense must be approved by you personally.

In any case, select and subscribe to or purchase accounting software. This is one of the most important first steps in business and it is especially important to set it up correctly from the beginning. One of the most popular is QuickBooks. There are others, of course, and some electronic medical records (EMR) companies (see below) provide accounting functionality with their systems. Whatever you choose, it will be particularly important when you are setting up your pharmacy inventory. These programs will track your inventory, allow you to order supplements, create invoices for patients, store credit card information securely, and more. In addition, you can usually generate all the reports you will need.

Subscribe to an electronic medical records (EMR) system.

Cloud-based electronic medical records (EMR) software is essential to the practice of medicine. If you're unfamiliar with the advantages, you're in for a treat. You'll no longer need filing cabinets, which usually take up dozens if not hundreds of square feet. You can find any information you need with a quick search. Indexing is done for you. The benefits go on and on.

Finding the right EMR for you takes time. There are numerous options. A good place to start is to consider an EMR system such as Power2Patient, Charm, Kareo, and Athenahealth, each of which is designed specifically for an integrative practice.

What should you look for?

- e-prescribing, and not just prescription faxing
- refill tracking for prescriptions
- accommodation for multiple providers to share a patient chart note
- the ability to load handouts

- a safe and secure patient-messaging system
- the ability to order supplements
- the ability to track labs
- a system that built to include alternative therapies, not one with a workaround to let you put them in as if they were conventional medical records
- online scheduling

Before you buy, test drive each system you consider. If possible, try it out in a colleague's office, not just with the setup that the rep provides. These systems are expensive but they're worth it. You'll invest time learning how to use the EMR, but it will be worth it in the time you save later, and all the conveniences you gain that will quickly become "must haves."

Take your time with this decision so you get it right the first time. If you have to switch systems, you'll probably encounter high fees for transferring your data across systems and formats, and some systems don't allow data porting at all.

Hire an attorney familiar with medical practices.

A good attorney is essential. They can draft documents you'll need that you cannot and should not write yourself such as intake signature pages, treatment consent, employment and partnership contracts. They can also advise you on legal aspects of certain business decisions. This is important because common sense can't always be your guide, as every locality has customs that are known only to those who already work around the courthouse, so to speak, and in the local or regional legal system. Investigate retainer arrangements and hourly rates.

Establish appropriate legal organization and licensure to do business.

You're not just a doctor now. You're the proprietor of a business. You'll probably need to incorporate or form some sort of legal entity, and you'll almost always need a business license of some kind. In most cases your attorney will guide you through this or take care of it on your behalf. Either way, make sure it gets done, and that you are meeting local and/or state requirements for the legal operation of a business apart from the issues associated with medical practice.

Find office space that is suited to the kind of work you'll be doing.

Start small if you must but think about where you can physically expand when you need more space in the future – because you will.

Our first practice was in a two-office suite with a kitchenette, an ADA-compliant restroom, plus a small reception area with an executive desk too big for the job, making it difficult to easily meet HIPPA standards for privacy. We used one office for patient visits, the other for physical exams and IV therapy. There wasn't room for both Steve and me to see patients at the same time, so we worked opposite days (plus one of us had to stay home to do childcare).

Within a year even that cramped arrangement was untenable. With no space to expand and no other vacancies to take over in the building, we stretched ourselves financially and moved to a bigger space in another location. Besides the problems that come with the physical move, we spent the next year re-directing people who somehow ended up at our old location. The lesson? Plan ahead – and assume growth.

As for reception, get the right kind of desk and arrangement of space that allows for privacy, a lesson we learned the hard way. And don't waste space on a big reception area. No one should have to wait too long in the first place, and if you're a cash practice your patients won't be in the mood to wait anyway.

If you're doing a pharmacy, think about space for storage, and consider whether you want a formal counter where patients can engage or if you just deal with delivery at the front desk.

Give your office manager their own office, too, and make it a private room. Your office manager is the hub of your clinic and they'll be there full time. Give them the room to work – also the privacy. This recognition of practical need is also an act of respect. It'll pay off for everyone.

If you intend to offer services such as massage, acupuncture, or something that requires special plumbing and electrical support (saunas, for instance), be sure the building will allow and support those services before you decide to add them, and be sure you have the physical space to accommodate them. Sometimes it's best to overbuy on square feet, use the space for something else in the meantime, then convert when the time finally comes.

Staff hangout space is important, too, perhaps a kitchenette or an area with a refrigerator, sink, and microwave, plus a small table or two and chairs. It is important for the staff to have a place to go when they need to step away but not too far away.

A side note: Covid taught Steve and me a lot about the possibilities of distance medicine. We had intended to expand our square footage by nearly half, but Covid showed us that with telemedicine we could be in the office less often, freeing up some space for the things we had planned for an expansion. Consider what must be done in person, what can be done online or via telemedicine, and factor that in as you decide how much space you need. State by state legalities around virtual visits also need to be considered here. Two doctors in the office every day need their own offices. But two doctors who come in a couple days each may be able to share a space, especially if it means significant financial savings for partners.

Consider accessibility. Wheelchair ramps are mandated in most localities, but there are exceptions for certain buildings. If you're above the first floor, you'll require an elevator. Be sure your location isn't the exception for accessibility. Once we thought it would be cute to have a practice in an old Victorian-style office. It had a garden for us to grow food in the summer (very naturopathic) and we could have had seating outside in the yard for patients and staff, all in service to that homey feeling that suits a naturopathic practice. Then we realized the cost to retrofit a place like this to accommodate all patients. Not a good fit.

Also consider what is often forgotten: does your potential location have nearby public transit and adequate parking? You have patients who need to park but your employees will need spaces, too. Plan for that.

Finally, this. Conserve your resources in general, your cash in particular. Don't spend on things you don't need. I'm talking about fancy fixtures, waiting-room furniture, and decorating. At this point if something doesn't directly bring in revenue, you can do without it. Remember, cash is king.

Create a complete set of prices.

Charge what your work is worth – and it's probably worth more than you think.

A lot of what we do in alternative medicine is education. When the focus is on teaching people what they want and need to know, you'll need longer visits and regular follow-up visits. People are paying to take care of their health and in many cases to get relief from pain and discomfort. It doesn't matter if you do that with a mechanical procedure, medicine, or advice. The outcome is still the same, and the outcome is what they're paying for.

That said, billing by the hour is rarely the best choice. If, say, a lawyer fixes a big problem with a five-minute phone call, it's unlikely they're going to bill you for five minutes. They're going to bill you for the benefit, though they may give the "service" a name and bill it out that way.

In the same way, your time is valuable because of what you provide, not just because you spent a little or a lot of time doing something. Give yourself permission to charge as you see fit, to give discounts for volume purchases, and to stick to your guns when people look for discounts without a profoundly good reason to grant them. (Besides, your patients should be focused on getting better, non on haggling. Patients who want to haggle are rarely the best patients you have.)

At the same time, be acquainted with reality. Check out your competitor's prices (ask around) and be sure you're in the ballpark. Charging a few bucks above the others won't knock you out of competition, and a few bucks below won't bring people racing to your door.

Factor in all the costs of a practice, not just your time. That means to factor in overhead including mortgage or rent for the space, consumables, staff salaries and benefits, utilities, subscriptions, retainers, services, fees, licenses, insurance, set-aside for savings, and anything else that's an expense for the practice. On top of that is where you add your own wage, what you want to make is weighed against what you can afford to charge.

The most painless way to do this calculation is to just do it. Collect your monthly expenses, divide them by the number of times you expect to perform each procedure in a month, then all that the foundational price for each procedure. Next, see how much you can add for your own profit. Now you're getting closer to your prices. Here's a partial list of procedures and services to get you started:

- Initial visit
- Return visit
- Procedure (a separate line for each procedure)
- Blood draw
- Pellet placements

- Monthly membership fee (if applicable/concierge)
- Record duplication
- Consult-by-phone
- After-hours consult

If you are selling supplements or prescriptions from an in-house pharmacy, price them, too, and do the same kind of calculation to get there. This time, though, start with the wholesale price of the product, then add the overhead, then add the profit.

Finally, consider whether you can increase prices because of a unique value you offer. Have you written a well-known book? Are you a public figure who gives talks or makes appearances on television? If there is something that makes you more attractive in any way over the competition, consider adding a premium to your prices to reflect that added benefit.

Decide if you will accept insurance or operate a cash practice.

Throughout this book I've used the term "cash practice" and "insurance practice." If you don't know what those terms mean, let's clear that up:

An insurance practice relies on payment from the insurance company. This takes a great deal of pressure and expense off your practice for billing and collection, but at the expense of having to make diagnoses and treatment under the limits the insurance company requires.

if you decline to accept insurance, you will be operating what's called a "cash practice," meaning your patients pay "out of pocket." They alone are responsible for payment. You can diagnose and prescribe as you like, and cash patients tend toward greater adherence and commitment. In addition, a cash practice will naturally attract people who chose you not because you accept their insurance but because they are dedicated to getting better. They are more likely to do what you say, especially in terms of changes in lifestyle. In fact, as we increased our prices over time, we noticed that more of our patients became more willing to work harder for their health.

Sounds like an easy choice to go with the cash practice, right? But a cash practice has challenges you may not have considered. In the next sections, I'll explain some of them.

Decide in advance how you will deal with delinquent payments.

It's nice to get paid without a middleman. It can be incredibly freeing to rid yourself of the strictures of insurance company limits on diagnosis and treatment. And as I said, the patients tend to be far more enthusiastic.

If only a cash practice were all such upsides.

Unless you demand payment at the time of treatment (and you can make that your policy if you like, though it comes with difficulties of its own), you will be responsible for sending out invoices and securing payment. This in turn means that when someone doesn't pay, you're responsible for dealing with the problem, too. You're going to have to decide how to deal with delinquent payments: for what amounts will you pay a percentage to a collection agency to secure your payment, and for what amounts will you follow up on your own – and how hard will you pursue if they continue to dodge the bill?

Here's a hard fact: when patients default on payments, it's unlikely you're going to get paid. It's too easy to dodge the payment and the consequences are minor. Patients can easily get a refund on a credit-card charge (that's called a "chargeback"), which can be the start of a time-consuming back-and-forth with the credit card company for you and your staff. Other patients are happy to ignore the collection agency. The numbers, at the time of this writing, go like this: there isn't much value in using a collection agency for bills under $200.

Plan how to deal with insurance patients who show up to a cash practice anyway.

Just because your clinic doesn't take insurance doesn't mean that insurance patients won't show up. The fact is they can still use their insurance by paying the bills themselves, then filing for reimbursement on their own. Now that you understand this, be sure that your patients understand this, too. You may gain a patient that you otherwise would lose.

That said, you still may have a decision to make. They are often going to need help from you to file, and to do prior authorizations. These tasks take time, either yours, that of support staff, or both. We're talking about phone calls, record searches, filling out forms, and engaging in correspondence.

Don't do this for free. In the beginning there is a lot of time for you to do this sort of thing. You'll probably want to because you want to help the patient as much as possible – but time is money. If you decide to offer this service, think about how you are going to pay for that service as it will become an overhead expense. As always, calculate the time and resource expense, add some amount for your own profit, and put it on the price list.

Decide how you will handle patients who cannot afford to pay.

It's difficult for some of us to accept that we can't just give away our services without costly consequences. Yet when you devalue your own time, those who pay for your time won't value it much, either. In fact, they won't always be serious about their own care. In a lecture in my first year of naturopathic medical school, a doctor stood before us and said, "If you came to medicine to help people, raise your hand," and of course we all raised our hands. Then he said, "If you plan to give pro-bono services or treat people without compensation, raise your hand," and most of us again raised our hands. Then he said something that's become a rule for my practice, and I suggest you make it one of your rules, too. He said, "Those that don't pay... won't do what you say."

I've seen it over and over: if you're not financially invested as a patient, you're probably not invested in any other way, either. My husband and I used to give free lectures at health food stores. We don't do that anymore. Why? The people who come out for our free advice fall into one of these categories: they ask lots of questions and never become patients, or they become patients and do not do what we prescribe.

There are of course cases of true and demonstrated hardship. In those cases we've sometimes made payment plans available, but we found that someone who can't afford treatment can't afford some of the basic elements of natural medicine such as the kinds of quality food that can make a difference in their health. So we weren't really helping them much at all.

Decide up front if you will see patients who can't pay your rates – and if you will see them, how much time you spend on them. Think about it in terms of time, resources, and dollars lost. How many hours a week will you spend on such patients? How much will that cost you? Do the usual calculations, though at this point you may be able to consult your price chart for the answers.

Also consider what you will do when a patient needs labs and cannot afford them, especially if labs are pass-along costs from outside firms whose services you pass through to patients.

Will you offer free service? Will you offer a discount? Will you offer extended payment plans?

It would be noble to offer free service to everyone who needs it, but if you did such a thing you couldn't pay your bills to keep the clinic open at all. Consider the balance that's right for you, then write down the policy.

One more thing: stick to the policy. You will often be tempted to make exceptions. Be careful with that. Each exception you allow makes the next one easier. Pretty soon you're in financial trouble – and then you can't help anyone at all.

Over time, meaning as your profitability becomes greater and more consistent, you can more easily give service to your community at no charge or find other ways to give back to those in need. But if you can't keep your practice up and running, you won't be serving those in need. You'll be the one in need.

Action Item: Prepare for Staff and Hire Them

Think about how the office will operate day to day.

Here are seven quick tips for hiring and for planning the daily operation of your office:

1. In a practice with two or more doctors, consider having one support staff person per physician. This may be a receptionist, an assistant, or someone with medical training. Whatever you do, prepare them to do what they're asked, because support staff need to be able to adapt to any situation and solve problems quickly. If a support person thinks any given task is beneath them, look for someone else. The task may indeed be beneath them, but in a start-up, everybody has to be prepared to do everything – and with a cheerful heart.

2. Do not hire friends or family. Do not hire anyone related to anyone who works in the clinic. Personal relationships will interfere with professional decisions and sour both.

3. Do background checks. I wish we had done more of them. People misrepresent themselves. That doesn't make them bad people, of course, but with the privacy

and sensitivity required in a doctor's office, it's not the place for trial runs or people who need extra monitoring. Patients are vulnerable when they see you. Protect them first, and protect your practice.

4. Put up cameras inside and outside, and feed them to a digital recording app. Theft happens – we've been stolen from more than once.

5. Lock your cash box. Make daily deposits.

6. Keep an inventory of your supplements, in real time if possible.

7. Require receipts from anyone who purchases anything for the practice, or on your behalf.

Draft an employee handbook.

Write down office policies. At least hit the basics: open and close times, open and close procedures, chain of command, emergency procedures, general obligations, expected behavior, break policies, vacation policies, dress code, and anything else you can think of that you want them to know. Your handbook may turn out to be a couple printed pages. That's fine, too. It's better to have something, even if it's small, than nothing.

People who work for you will do better if they receive an indication from the beginning that you are in charge, that you have thought about what you expect, and that these expectations are codified.

Create job descriptions.

Write descriptions for each job in your office. Be specific about responsibilities and expectations when you can, but also acknowledge that jobs evolve and change, especially in a new organization. This doesn't have to be exhaustive. It may be no more than a few lines. Be specific when you can, but when you're not sure, leave it. In this way you can make use of what you learn between setup time, when you have no experience running the practice, and weeks or months down the road, when the question arises. At that point you'll know more than you do now, and be equipped to make a better decision.

Decide whether each job should be full time or part time.

Your office manager needs to be full time or near-full time. The day-to-day operation of the clinic depends on them, and things are going to come up that you can't anticipate. You want someone in place to address these things, or head them off before they arise. You don't want to be faced with these things out of your busy day when you're with patients.

As for the rest of your employees, part-timers are best for a new practice. You typically have to provide benefits, including expensive insurance, to full-time employees. Plus full-timers who have to miss a day or two of work are not easy to fill in when they're gone, especially when last-minute absences arise with child care or illness. If you can hire two part-timers for each position, do so. Work with them to cover the time you need covered, and give them the flexibility to swap hours with approval from your manager.

Hire an office manager.

An office manager will operate your business on a daily basis. Pay them well and keep them happy. They will be your representative in day-to-day questions of business. They will be your eyes and ears into the practice. They will help with or take care of the things you cannot do or don't know how to do. You need someone you can trust completely and who will deal with things to your best advantage – a "mini-me," so to speak. Choose wisely. When you start looking for an office manager, look for these things:

- They understand the work you do and they believe in it.
- They are good at working independently but they also take direction well.
- They have at least some experience working in a medical practice.
- They have basic knowledge of HIPPA.
- They have basic knowledge of human resources responsibilities, especially in terms of foundational legal obligations, and they have a plan for interacting with and managing the professional behavior of employees.
- They have excellent customer service skills.

- They lead a healthy lifestyle. (They represent your clinic. They need to demonstrate your mission in the way they look and act.)
- They can troubleshoot basic computer problems.
- They are interested in staying for a long time.
- Make sure you background check and always check in with references, professional and personal.

What happens in your practice affects how patients, colleagues, and the community perceive you as a person. This depends on how good a job your manager does. A good office manager will create a structure in which they run the business to your satisfaction and insulate you from all but the most critical issues; this allows you to focus on what you do best, the practice of medicine.

As the clinic grows, this segregation of responsibility becomes more and more important, because there will be more and more office-driven business to deal with. In the beginning you will have more time to be involved in the business side of things. You'll also be concerned about handing over key responsibilities to anyone other than yourself. It's important to recognize this tendency and make a purposeful effort to leave more and more things to the manager, and check in less and less frequently until you are able to "leave it to the system," meeting each week with your manager at a scheduled time to deal with the week's recap and to handle any decisions that need making but that did not require an immediate reply.

In other words, the sooner you learn to let your manager do their job, the sooner your office will run smoother and with less worry on your part. A good manager will help you stay in practice longer and prevent burnout.

One more thing: since your office manager will be focused on working with staff, your manager should be hired first, then made a significant part of the hiring process. If you have high confidence in your manager early on, you should let them do the hiring themselves, with final approval from you.

Hire a receptionist (or two).

If there's one job besides yours that has to be filled without question every day, it's the person at the front of the office who answers the phone and greets patients. If you can at all, hire two part-timers. This gives you someone to call on when the scheduled receptionist can't come in.

Make sure your receptionists present a good example of what your practice is all about. They should be friendly, in good health, patient, and skilled at doing several things at once. A private clinic ought to provide an exceptional experience. Your staff should be exceptional, and your receptionists are the tip of the spear.

When you are somehow stuck without a receptionist, deal with the challenge promptly. Send your phones to voicemail with a message explaining that the message will be checked within the hour and someone will call back (and that if this is an emergency the caller should hang up and dial 911). Temp agencies are expensive, prohibitively so. Avoid them.

Hire medical support staff.

Medical support staff such as Nurses, MA, phlebotomists and EMT's may be essential for your practice depending on the services you have. Depending upon the state law of the state you set your practice up in, often, an MA can be trained to do anything legally if it is in the scope of practice of the one delegating. An MA can be hired at a lower wage than a nurse or EMT. On the other hand, the formal emergency training and skills of these trained licenses is often worth it. You have to pay for those with greater degrees to stay and with the skills they have it is usually worth the investment.

Decide what wages and benefits you want to offer.

Focus first on wages, because you may not have full-time employees at the beginning and you may use all part-timers for a long time. Pay above minimum wage. Consider the cost of living in your area. Be as generous as you can afford to be. Whether full- or part-time, most candidates for a job are primarily focused on what is to them the bottom line, which is how much money they will take home each week. Good pay creates an incentive not just to do a good job but also to stick around, and turnover is expensive and troublesome, not to mention the gnawing effect it can have on reputation and the tendency of patients to stick with you over time.

Next, consider perks. You might offer them discounts or wholesale rates on supplements. Consider giving them free or discounted office visits and/or treatments, again up to a certain limit per month or year. You might even extend this to a spouse. Offer paid days off for wellness, pregnancy, bereavement, or just as a bonus. Create incentives to sell supplements by offering a commission. (Be careful how you structure this. The desire to make extra money can cause even thoughtful employees to shift to the "hard sell" at moments that may be inappropriate, and that will reflect poorly on the practice and on you.) Set up a break room and stock it with complimentary snacks and drinks, and make the area look attractive and special. Take them all out for a nice lunch or dinner once a quarter, or even once a month. Offer gifts for staying in a position for a period time – an iPad, for instance, at the first anniversary is an impressive gift, and an impressive incentive. Be creative in all these things but remember that even small things can have a big impact. People want to know you appreciate them. Be sure they hear it from you in ways big and small.

In terms of compensation beyond the paycheck, we promote healthy living for our employees so we give paid wellness days, time off for personal needs with great latitude for what is permitted, bereavement leave, and the elevation of certain unpaid days off to paid days off after a year of service. If you have full-time employees, work with your office manager to choose appropriate benefits, mainly insurance and more time off than part-timers receive. Consider the tax implications of these benefits as well, because they can be significant.

Finally, keep in mind this general rule: you have to treat employees the same. You can't have one set of rules for your favorites and another set of rules for the rest. Besides, regardless of what the law requires, employees talk with each other. Don't expect them to be in the dark for long about everyone else's benefits or salary. That's a formula for trouble – for you. With that in mind, be transparent and precise – and consistent – in what you provide your employees in terms of pay, time off, maternity leave, vacation, sick-day policy, work reviews (in terms of frequency, content, and consequences), and what constitutes a firing offense.

We learned the hard way. When we launched, we told our employees that they could have performance reviews if they wished – it was not required, just an option. Pretty soon, though, every employee decided to ask for a performance review because they decided (with little evidence, by the way), that these reviews would be accompanied by pay increases. The news that these increases were not a part of every review was met with disappointment at best and lingering frustration at worst.

So set clear boundaries, definitions, procedures, and expectations. Do this to avoid unnecessary conflict, whose ramifications can go in every unpleasant direction.

Make a plan for keeping connected with your manager and staff.

Meet with your business manager every week. Meet at least monthly for one on ones with the other doctors in your practice. Put these meetings on the calendar and don't skip them, not ever. They need to become a part of the way you practice. If you treat these meetings like "if we have time" events instead of unbreakable appointments, your ability to steer the practice the way you want it to go will fade quickly.

Make these meetings a two-way street. Listen. Ask questions. Respond honestly and reflectively to what your people say. If you don't have answers to questions, say so, then come back to folks in a timely way with what they need to know.

Do the same for employees. For most matters, their first contact should be your manager. But they also will appreciate and deserve a formal setting to tell you what's on their mind, for you to tell them what you're thinking, and for you to give them encouragement and kudos for the work they do. An open-door policy to your office is a good thing, but not without suggestions about what is for a meeting versus what is for a "pop in."

Ask your employees for their input on how to make the clinic better. Work with your manager to assign special or unique tasks to individuals. This empowers the staff. Everyone wants to feel important and a part of the team.

Just as important is the tone of all this. Show up with an agenda that's written down, even if it's just "tell me what you've done this week," "here's what I've done," and "here's what I see coming next week." This meeting will set the tone for the practice overall and your leadership in particular – and how seriously your employees and partners take your direction. You don't have to be a spectacular leader, you just have to show up, be patient, demonstrate that you have a plan, and be firm about it. If you lead, people will follow – so lead.

Action Item: Begin Marketing and Branding

Set up your online presence.

You're going to need social media accounts, email at your own domain, and a website. You're also going to need someone to set up, monitor, and maintain them. Plus you'll need someone to post on your accounts to give you a social media presence.

Website

You can hire someone to set up your web presence and build your site. You can spend a lot or a little, but as with most things you get what you pay for. Consider doing it yourself. The systems now available for doing it yourself are quite professional and can make you look great online (though you typically will not look unique – keep that in mind, if it matters to you). You can build your own website and purchase a domain name (the address at which people find you on the Internet) on your own. Companies to guide you through it are many and varied and quite reliable, even if you're not technically inclined. (Check out GoDaddy or Wix, for instance.) Pick a domain name, typically your clinic name @ .com. If your clinic name isn't available as a domain, consider simple variations such as appending the name of the town you're in, or adding the word "My" or "Visit." Not sure of the name you'll use?

Buy several domains for a year lock-in. They're cheap, about $12 each.

Get that website online as soon as you can. Not yet sure of the physical address of your practice? Don't worry – just put "coming soon" and give them what you do have, such as your email address and your mission statement, logo, tagline, and list of offered services.

Website Sales and Appointments

Consider too whether you're going to sell supplements online as well as from your office. You might also allow people to set their own appointments using an online calendar. If you offer other services such as massage, you might allow online appointments for that as well. In those cases, you'll almost certainly need a web professional to establish and monitor the system. In addition, many EHR programs have embedded online scheduling. Again, don't take on that role yourself. You may be able to find time for the basics but what you're paying for with a professional is their availability when you are doing the main thing you're paid to do, being a doctor and running a clinic.

Email

Set up email addresses. Establish one for yourself using your name but for the rest go with generic titles, not people's names: reception@SiteName.com, info@SiteName.com, manager@SiteName.com, and so forth. If you want to personalize them later, you can.

Webmaster

You need a designated webmaster, too; someone you can call in the middle of the day if your email system fails or your site gets hacked. Avoid taking the role yourself even if you know what you're doing. Your time is more economically spent being a doctor, not a web guru.

Social Media

Set up social media accounts for the practice. You'll almost certainly want to have a Facebook page, but there are many platforms whose popularity rises and falls, and new platforms appear all the time. The value of social media is that you can be part of an ongoing conversation. This in turn helps keep you top of mind for people who may want the services you offer.

The downside is that you have to dedicate resources to being a part of that ongoing conversation, meaning someone has to post on your behalf every day. That post can't be simple advertising – "Come to my clinic!" is not a post that's going to help you, and it will in fact make you look tone deaf and selfish. Posts that get traction are posts that add value to the conversation out of your personal expertise: tips for healthy living, advice on how to eat right, exercise ideas, mindfulness guidance, and so on. Designate someone to post every day on your behalf and give them resources they can scan for ideas. Often your webmaster offers these services. You can arm them with articles or health tidbits and they can post on your behalf each week from this pool of information.

Plan for marketing and advertising.

Here's an old joke: a guy opens a business. His friends and neighbors cheer him on. A month later he had to shut down for lack of customers. On the last day, he sat down for a consolation drink with the folks who had been there at the beginning. "I don't get it," said the former business operator. "This business had exactly what this town has been asking for, yet I opened the doors and no one showed up. Even all of you! You folks want what I had to offer, but none of you came by even once."

Came the reply: "You never asked."

Patients don't just show up when you open the door. You have to let them know you're there and you're open, and you have to invite them.

That means you have to advertise. That does *not* mean you need to start spending a lot (or even much of anything) on advertising.

If you're participating in social media, you may be doing all you need. It can be powerful. As for formal advertising, be careful.

Minimize spending. If you can avoid spending anything at all, avoid spending anything at all. If you decide to spend, do your homework. Compare the cost of an advertising campaign (e.g., a sign on a bench or renting a billboard) with how much work it will take to pay for it – not just dollars and cents, but number of appointments and hours of work, less the expense of doing the work in terms of support staff, utilities, and supplies. It's a simple decision: there must be a return on your investment or it's a waste of resources.

Meet people. It's the most powerful way to establish community presence. Get to know hairdressers, folks who do nails, massage therapists – anyone who spends time with lots of people. Check in with real estate agents, too. They often provide gift baskets whose main value is telling new residents what services are available. They may welcome a brochure from your clinic that they can include.

Know your demographic. Who goes to the doctor the most? In fact, women do. Aging men visit often, too. Parents bring their teenagers and people in health crises come in. On the other hand, college students and athletes do not spend much money at all on healthcare. When you are designing advertising and choosing target media, keep these things in mind.

Print up leave-behinds – stickers, cards, brochures – that you can give to people, leave in places that welcome them, and give to patients in your office to get your name on display where they'll see it in their home. Go heavy on photos – people are attracted to photos – and use your logo. Get professional pictures, too. Don't just grab the last few clicks off your iPhone.

Finally, establish a weekly goal for advertising and promotion and do that one thing a week. It doesn't have to be big, but the consistency of weekly activity will add up to increased business.

PART IV: How to Keep Your Practice (and Yourself) Healthy and Successful

In this section, I'll share what I've done over the last two decades to sustain our practice and ourselves.

Kelly's Experience

It has been 17 years since we first opened the doors to our clinic, NatureMed. We began with one treatment room and two doctors, Steve and I. Today we have six doctors and seven support staffers. NatureMed is bigger than ever, and our vision continues to grow, along with our ambition. There have been times when we felt we might not make it, but we've weathered all storms. Many things have kept us going personally and professionally, but it all flows from what we decided early on would be our highest priorities, taking care of our practice, taking care of ourselves, and serving our patients the way we would want to be served.

Steve and I have worked purposefully and explicitly to stay well connected not only as spouses but also as co-equal professionals in practice together. It's vital for professional partners in a practice to share their concerns, to work through problems together, and to stop and appreciate successes as they occur. In addition, we have supported one another in taking care of our own health, and prioritized carving out time to do so.

Our connection with our staff has been another key to success. Every employee plays an important role in the success of a clinic. We honor the significance of the receptionist and our manager as representing us, our values and the demands of the job. We know that patients can treat staff with less respect than they show to the doctors. People who work at the front desk have to put up with a lot. They're a patient's first encounter with the clinic, so our staffers have a lot on their shoulders, and they have to be kind and patient even when it's not easy. To support them, we host a gathering twice each year outside of work for staff and their significant others. It lets us get to know each other better and reminds us of how much we have in common – it keeps us connected, and we believe the best way to stay connected is to work at it. We invite staff input on how the office can be improved, and we maintain an open-door policy so staff can tell us what's on their mind anytime. We make sure they know we're grateful for all their feedback, positive or negative. It's always valuable to hear from colleagues whom we know want the best for all of us.

Still in many ways we're a small office, and that's how we like it. We feel connected to each other even as we recognize that there is a hierarchy of responsibility and obligation. We know the boundaries and we honor each other by honoring those boundaries. It made for a satisfying and successful journey.

Which brings me to this, the last section. Here are some thoughts and plans to consider once your practice is up and running. Think about them in advance, for sure, but come back to this section once your clinic is on track. The things I've shared up to this point are mostly to help you get started. The things in this part are mostly to help you stay on the right path.

How to Use This Section

While the previous sections of this book are written explicitly to help you in anticipation of launching your practice, this portion is focused on what you can do to stay in business and enhance your business once the practice is underway. That doesn't mean you can't and shouldn't read it now. This part will give you some insight as to what and how you ought to think about day-to-day practice. It's good to consider this before those days arrive.

You've probably been making notes and taking action based on what you've read so far, especially in the previous section. Consider this final section a guide to planning your immediate future – a way to think about your practice on an ongoing basis once the foundational elements are in place and up and running. Feel free to add these to your plan now and flesh them out accordingly. No need to wait!

Show up.

Here's an uncanny truth: the more you show up for your practice, the more patients come in the door. If you planned to see patients on Monday from 9-5 but there is only one patient scheduled, stay at work anyway.

Your presence opens the clinic to opportunity.

In our experience, those slow days often fill up, and quickly, when patients start calling in looking for a last-minute opening. A one-patient day can quickly turn into a full slate, but you have to be there to do the work.

Set up your schedule and show up whether you have patients on the calendar or not. You never know what your presence alone will make possible.

This also has a positive effect on the way business is conducted, and how employees and associates do their jobs. As your practice grows, so does the temptation to delegate more than you should. When you have an amazing office manager and strong support staff, it's easy to become complacent.

Don't let that happen. You have to show up.

Even if you're not needed as much as you used to be, show up anyway. Keep up your weekly meetings with your manager, and your one-on-ones with your associates or hired medical staff. Remember, when the boss is away, the mice will play!

Things will get out of control if you take advantage of a well-running machine by not showing up.

Deal with disgruntled patients right away.

Disgruntled patients can ruin your practice and zap your enthusiasm for practicing medicine. I once had a husband and wife come in for an extended, comprehensive visit. I gave them everything they asked for: physical exam, extensive blood work, nutritional counseling, supplement recommendations, and plenty of extra attention. In the end, they did a chargeback on their credit card and wrote up a bad review on social media telling anyone who would read it that we had not met their needs. I didn't know what to do, so I didn't do anything.

Now I know better.

Patients can feel disappointed, angry, frustrated, or ripped off for lots of reasons that have nothing to do with the care you provide. Maybe they found the receptionist to be brusque. Maybe they couldn't find a parking space right away. Maybe someone in the waiting area was laughing too loudly for their tastes. Or maybe they just woke up on the wrong side of the bed. Oftentimes it is more about them rather than what your clinic has done to them, but that is not what they see.

When the recipient of their hostility is you, it doesn't matter what the cause of their bad feeling turns out to be. Now it's your problem. And bad news travels fast. (And in a cash practice, people writing checks on the spot don't hesitate to refuse to pay at all, and to tell anyone who will listen about their complaint.)

Do this: follow up with each patient at the end of the visit, as I described elsewhere in this book. Make this a front-office task and make it an inviolable priority. Give every patient a chance to offer praise and complaints – in a formalized, sit-down, and brief session – so you can deal with any issues on the spot, and before they get outside the walls of your clinic. Word of mouth can make or break a practice. It's mostly a game of prevention.

If you find out there's a problem after the patient has left, call them to try to fix it. Call as soon as possible. Take on the task yourself so it's clear that this is a priority – you may wish to tell the patient that you are so concerned that you made it your personal priority instead of leaving it to other staff. This can save you a lot of trouble. Just that acknowledgement and care can shift their action from potentially going on the internet and bad mouthing you to feeling that they want to stay in your practice. They may even become more committed to you.

In every case, stick with it until the patient tells you, in words, that they are satisfied. It's worth the expense in resources.

Treat your staff as you would like to be treated.

Your staff have a lot of responsibility. If they do a poor job, the worst that can happen to them is you can fire them.

But the worst that can happen to you is that your practice can suffer damage in the form of lost patients, lost revenue, diminished reputation, or even going out of business.

By all means, treat your staff well because it's the right thing to do. They deserve to have jobs they enjoy, a boss who listens, and a daily experience that makes them pleased to come into work.

But remember too that treating them well is also the wise thing to do.

They're handling a lot of things on your behalf, in your name, many times in your stead, and when you're not around. What they do and how they do it reflects on you and has a direct impact on your future and your bottom line. Consider, for instance, the work of your receptionist. The position of receptionist at an integrative clinic is not like any old medical reception position. They need to know about what you do, what integrative medicine is, what you do when you're with patients, how you can help them, in what matters you can help them – all this in addition to regular reception duties. It's important to arm them with the experience of being a patient. Bring them in and teach them so that they can represent you honestly.

Give them a reason to do their jobs well. Let them know how important they are not just to you but to the business. Show them their value by giving them respect and consideration. Be patient. Be kind. And be engaged. When they're upset about something, treat them the way you treat disgruntled patients: be open, be proactive, and stick with it until the problem is solved.

Schedule "CEO Time" to consider the future of your clinic.

Continue to stretch yourself and your practice with ideas for growth. Don't fall asleep at the wheel. If your clinic isn't growing in terms of patients and offerings, it will soon be shrinking.

Where do these new ideas come from? I suggest opening a "note page" on your phone and writing down ideas when they come to you. Did you see a TV show or read an article describing some new treatment? Has there been a recent breakthrough in a clinical trial of some kind? Is there a fad in treatment that needs promoting – or debunking? Any idea you have that's related to your practice, write it down.

Here's how to act on all that: once a week, schedule a meeting with yourself and/or your business partner, about 20 minutes. Go through the list and consider what you might do to change, add to, or improve your practice based on those ideas. You don't have to go through all of them, and you don't have to settle on a firm yes or now. But look at them seriously, and think in terms of what you want your practice to be and what you are capable of doing. By writing things down throughout the week, you spare yourself the impossible task of being creative on demand – and on-the-spot creativity is nearly impossible.

As you go through this material, speak with your partners or trusted advisors about what they think might work. Then, for those ideas that continue to appeal and that stand up to research, write down plans for implementation. Since you already have a weekly "CEO Time" meeting on your calendar, that time you spend will gradually be divided among looking ahead and actually doing things to grow into the future.

Keep in mind that failure is often a step toward progress.

Know this: many of the things you'll try will not go the way you hope. I'm talking about partnerships, new marketing initiatives, experiments in balancing work and home, interacting with colleagues who have experience to share, financial plans – you want them to work but some of them are going to fail, maybe most of them.

Don't let it discourage you! Failure is what happens when you're trying to succeed. In fact, that's the very definition of the path to progress. It's the definition of science itself: you try out your best guess, you learn from where and how it falls short, then you try again.

Failure is the pavement on the road to success. Be grateful for the failures, because they are your education. And keep your eye on the goal.

Over the years, we have experienced failures in many ways. We had failed advertising campaigns, seminars, clinic systems, partners, equipment promotions, and various health programs. Each one of these gave us direction about where we wanted to go and what would work. In many cases, we felt that if someone had told us up front how to do a certain thing, or what not to do at all, we would have saved lots of time and money. Helping you in just this way is one of the main things that inspired me to write this book.

Yet no matter how much you know, failure is part of the path and part of the plan. Be ready for it, and learn from it.

Know your patients before
they come in the door.

When a patient comes in for a visit, you have a responsibility to be prepared to deal with them on a personal and specific basis. It's an ethical and professional obligation. It's necessary in order to do your job well. That said, it's also respectful – and smart business.

On a first visit your patient will fill out intake paperwork. They didn't enjoy filling it out and if you asked for it you need to have a reason. So read it. If you don't read it, don't refer to it, or ask questions that were already answered on the page, patients have a right to ask why you had them spend time on it – and whether you are all that interested in their concerns in the first place.

Our intake paperwork at NatureMed is lengthy. In addition to symptoms, we dig deep for PMHx, FmHx, HxPI, dietary recalls, and more. I review this before we sit down together, and as I go through it with them I ask questions to get more information that I will need. When they question my questions, often saying something like, "Well, I already wrote that down," I thank them and tell them that I would like to hear a little more from them personally. Engaging with them in this kind of way provides a powerful signal to them that you care about their health and their outcomes.

Finally, make a note in the chart about something memorable about the patient. Perhaps they mention an upcoming graduation or personal achievement, a job promotion, or some point of pride. Note it, then ask about it the next time you meet with them. These kinds of genuine connections will increase their confidence in you and increase their interest in doing what you ask.

Check your ego – and listen.

It's easy to come out of school feeling like you know just about everything you need to know. If you're a specialist, if you attended a school with a high profile or grand reputation, or if you did a prestigious residency, that feeling is even more likely to come over you. It's good to have confidence, but as in everything else too much self-regard is not good for you as a person. And in our line of work, it will cloud your judgment and send your patients elsewhere.

When a patient is coming to you for health advice, keep in mind that although you are the doctor and you have the medical expertise they need, the patient is the one who has been living in the body that you're examining. They're the one who has been feeling the pain and doing their best to accommodate whatever is happening to them. In short, they've been on the front lines of this very personal experience a lot longer than you have.

Therefore, they are not just recipients in the process of treatment and diagnosis. They are participants. They bring value. To ignore this fact is to fail to provide the best environment for healing.

So check your ego – and listen.

It is important to ask a patient what they think the problem might be, and what they feel about the state of their health. I ask this even when they present with multiple and complex symptoms because their priorities can point me in the right direction as I try to analyze what they're going through. Intuition is a valuable thing in diagnosis and validating the patient's perspective and opinion can enhance the process.

It's fine if you don't know all the answers, or if you find yourself stumped early on. You can't know everything. And it's fine to be unfamiliar with some diagnosis or treatment they mention that you've never heard of. It's perfectly reasonable for you to say that you don't know what it is they've mentioned, and that you'll do some research and get back to them.

During my last year of medical school, one of my first patients in clinic was an 80-year-old female. I will never forget sitting across from her and feeling like a child, relative to her long life and experience. I asked myself how I might possibly help someone who had been on this earth so much longer than I, and who had seen so much more.

So I did the thing I knew to do: I listened. I stayed focused on her medical concerns, I processed what she had to say and let my interest and curiosity lead me to connections between what she needed and the medical knowledge I possessed.

In the clinic, they used to say, "Fake it 'til you make it." I say, "You don't have to fake it. Just listen – then follow what you hear toward the answer."

Treat your patients' time with respect.

Don't make patients wait.

Show up on time. Give them the time they need. And schedule them so you have time to do exactly that. When patients sense that you're in a hurry, or, worse, that you're trying to rush them, they feel disrespected.

That's because they're being disrespected – by their doctor.

That is bad for your reputation, bad for your practice, and bad for starting and maintaining a trusting relationship.

You expect your patients to plan their day so that they arrive on time. You are so committed to this that you probably charge them for missed appointments. And when patients abuse your time and goodwill, you resent it. They feel the same when you do that to them. Prioritize your patients' time by planning your days carefully, and with appropriate "padding" to allow everyone to have the time they paid for. (Remember that in a cash practice they are paying out of their own pockets – and if they feel disrespected they'll let you know by telling you out-right or by taking their business elsewhere.)

Keep healthy.

Let me make a prediction: at the start of your launch, and for a long time after, you're going to burn that candle at both ends. You'll promote yourself and your clinic, you'll go above and beyond for every patient, you'll work to impress the community of providers that you're now a part of, and when you have spare time you'll spend it on building up your business.

All those things are reasonable – smart, even. You want to do well and a solid future is built on a solid beginning.

But keep this in mind: you remember what they tell you on airplanes, right? They say *in the event of an emergency, put the mask on yourself before helping others.* That's because it's nearly impossible to do your best for others until you've taken care of yourself.

So take care of yourself.

I realize it's hard to do. It's instinct: doctors take care of others *before* taking care of themselves. I was no different. In the beginning of our practice, I was a new mother. I had no money to pay for childcare. I saw patients three days a week while Steve watched the baby. On the other days I stayed home and Steve went to the clinic. Occasionally we'd luck into family or friends to look after our daughter. When that happened we didn't use the break for a mental health day, we both went into our tiny office and worked.

The one luxury I had I came to see was not a luxury but a necessity. I had the flexibility to create my own schedule. Exercise gave me sanity and kept me healthy physically, mentally, and emotionally. I joined a gym and on my few days off I would take our daughter with me and check her in to the free daycare while I got my exercise.

On the days I worked I woke up early and did a 30- to 45-minute workout video. If I felt too stressed to work, I took the day off – not often, but when necessary. On the weekends I negotiated time with Steve to exercise and to cover one another. I was constantly multi-tasking, but I was doing the bare minimum at least: exercise, eating healthy, and getting to bed on time.

In hindsight I realize that I could have and should have taken more three-day weekends, or one week off every three months.

So take care of yourself. Create the clinic, the schedule, and the lifestyle you want. Find your bare minimum and prioritize that so that you can take care of yourself. Don't compromise on your desires, goals, and limits. When what you need to stay satisfied comes into conflict with outside demands (or pressure you put on yourself), give yourself permission to say no – then say it: no.

Think about how you want your days to proceed and what you want your life to look like, then reject those things that don't bring you closer to making them happen.

Afterword

The Work Begins

This book is a trip down the path I took from my first thoughts about opening a clinic all the way through our first day of practice and beyond. You'll find some of your own story in here, along with your doubts, your worries, and I hope some of your excitement. The anticipation and satisfaction of opening your own integrative practice are great feelings. There is stress, of course, and lots of hard work, but it's manageable if you prepare for it – and nothing great ever comes without setting yourself to a task and sticking to it no matter what.

Opening NatureMed was a fulfillment of a dream that began before I even knew it was what I would want. My journey to natural medicine began when I was five years old. My identical twin sister and I had been born with a hereditary ureter defect. By the time we had corrective surgery, the problem had grown to the point of having damaged kidneys. Living in Boulder, Colorado in the 1970s, our mother sought out alternative therapy. She took us to the only naturopathic doctor in town. From that day forward I was brought up on brown bread and carrot sticks and no red meat. Raised primarily by my mother who was on a spiritual quest, this also meant a primary vegetarian diet and regular meditation practice (which I rebelled against and during which I almost always fell asleep).

When we were 14, mom moved us to the Malakoff Diggins area of northern California. She had no money but with that came motivation to take an opportunity: she had been asked to serve for a year as the caretaker of a home there. Just prior we had been living in the Bay area and she wanted to get us out of the city to a place she thought we would be more fulfilling, not to mention safer. It was here that my vision for life began to take shape for the first time. We occupied an otherwise beautiful home with no electricity, no hot water, and an outhouse for a bathroom. We were in the middle of a community of committed poets. It was what I call my first "wilderness experience," and it was in those months that I came to realize that my life would need to be connected to nature itself and natural living.

In those days I learned to live with nothing, but in that I found everything. That quest has defined my life ever since.

Whatever path through life has brought you to the point of considering your own practice, your story is at the heart of why you make the choices you make, just as my story has guided the path you've read about here.

Now the work begins: the work of shifting from the way you've been practicing our discipline into a more independent, more goal-centered, and more satisfying existence, both personally and professionally. You have goals to ponder, choices to make, things to bring into your life and things to eliminate.

There will be mental work and physical labor, risks to assess and chances to take.

If you need something to hang onto when the times get tough, hang on to this: it's worth it. Take it from someone who's been there – take it from someone who's on the same path as you, who's seen where you'll be going, and who knows that for those who commit themselves, it's going to be okay.

You have a special gift and if you've made it to this point in my book, you've demonstrated the passion you'll need to see this through.

All good things to you, then. Enjoy the work and enjoy the trip!

END

Are you thinking of launching an integrative practice?

Want to go beyond this book?

Want consulting and advice directly from the author?

Visit
IntegrativePracticeConsultant.com.

ACKNOWLEDGEMENTS

Writing this book has long been a goal of mine and I am pleased to share it with you, but the ideas here are hardly all my own.

Thanks to my husband, Steve, who has given so much encouragement and support to write this book, and whose business acumen was key to our success when we launched NatureMed on a wing and a prayer (and a tiny bank account) so many years ago.

Thanks to my kids, Brianna and Wesley, who would allow me to vent about writing this book at the dinner table and during trips to the bus stop.

To my father, David Jacobs, who always encouraged me to follow my passion and who showed me by example that I should take all parts of entrepreneurism in stride – and always be patient. He gave me the wisdom to manage and run a business with integrity, and with respect for others.

To my mother, Faye Jacobs, who taught me how to have courage and to be a strong woman with an open heart for the world.

ACKNOWLEDGEMENTS

To my siblings, who are all entrepreneurs, and who have given me advice along the way or shared stories to help get through various crossroads.

And finally, to Michael Long, my writing coach in this project. He helped me assemble my thoughts into the book you now hold in your hands.

ABOUT THE AUTHOR

Kelly J. Parcell, ND, has been in private practice for two decades. She earned her doctorate in naturopathic medicine from Bastyr University in Seattle, Washington. She is a member of the Colorado Association of Naturopathic Doctors as well as the American Association of Naturopathic Physicians. She comes from an athletic family and is enthusiastic about nearly everything related to sports and health.

www.ingramcontent.com/pod-product-compliance
Lightning Source LLC
Chambersburg PA
CBHW071208210326
41597CB00016B/1730